Shaking up Shakespeare

Also by Natalie Muller

Fiction

Poisoning The Nest

Non Fiction

Black Cockie Press 12 Week Novel Writing Masterclass Workbook:

A complete first draft in 12 weeks.

Shaking up Shakespeare

Natalie Muller

Black Cockie Press

Shaking up Shakespeare
Published by Black Cockie Press
21 Camp Street Katoomba NSW
http://www.blackcockiepress.com.au

Copyright © Natalie Muller 2023
Character images © Adam Muller 2022
Cover design © Natalie Muller 2023
Distributed by IngramSpark
Printed by IngramSpark
ISBN: 9780645489644

The moral right of the author has been asserted
National Library of Australia
Cataloguing-in-publication entry:
Muller, Natalie
Shaking up Shakespeare
Non Fiction
ISBN: 9780645489644

All rights reserved. Except as permitted under the Australian copyright act of 1968 (for example, a fair dealing for the purpose of study, research, criticism or review), no part of this publication may be reproduced, stored in or introduced into a database and retrieval system or transmitted in any form or any means (electronic, mechanical, photocopying, recording or otherwise) without the prior written permission of both the owner of copyright and the above publishers.

Although the author and publisher have made every effort to ensure that the information in this book was correct at press time, the author and publisher do not assume and hereby disclaim any liability to any party for any loss, damage, or disruption caused by errors or omissions, whether such errors or omissions result from negligence, accident, or any other cause.

To "Sweetie".

Contents

Introduction 9

How to use this book 12

Meet the Upstart Crow.
Introducing Shakespeare Year 8 Unit 13
Henry IV Part 1. Year 10 Unit 149
Julius Caesar. Year 10 Unit 177
The Taming of the Shrew. Year 10 Unit 205
Year 10 Unit Essay Writing Lessons 233

Program Template Year 8 Unit 257
Program Template Year 10 Unit 259

Bibliography 261

Glossary of Shakespearean terms and words 263

About the Author 267

Introduction.

This is the book I wanted and needed when I started teaching.

This book will change how you see Shakespeare.

Two years ago when I sat down to write this book, a task that I optimistically hoped would take six months, I was horrified to find what was being produced for teachers to teach Shakespeare and his plays.
Resources that were dull; or dumbed-down ignorant of the latest scholarship in the field, misquoting centuries old stories and anecdotes. In the past twenty years, scholarship has moved on from trying to find the 'Holy Grail' of a text actually written in Shakespeare's own hand, to understanding the world in which Shakespeare lived and worked.
Placing Shakespeare, not as an isolated genius, but as a writer, actor and theatre shareholder in a world of many theatres, many actors and many writers. With the knowledge that Shakespeare was writing his plays for a specific space, and the constraints of audience expectation. His knowledge of his fellow actor's strengths, weaknesses and demands as performers, gives us and in turn our students a much more dynamic vision of the plays, and the man who wrote them.

This book contains four complete units of work. One introduction to Shakespeare unit, written for Stage 4 or year 8 students. And units of work on three complete plays, written for Stage 5 or year 10 students.

The Introduction to Shakespeare Unit seeks to place Shakespeare, the man, into his cultural and historical context as well as familiarising students with the language of the plays themselves. No complete play is studied in this unit, rather students learn how The Elizabethan theatre world operated, how playwrights collaborated and competed with each other. How playwrights fitted into the theatrical world and how the theatres themselves functioned. This unit challenges traditional methods of teaching Shakespeare, by providing a context for his work. Rather than deifying Shakespeare as a solo voice providing content for the Elizabethan theatre world, students understand what made him special in a very cutthroat (sometimes literally) world. Students in this way begin to understand why Shakespeare's plays are the ones that are remembered, and the plays of one of his biggest rivals and influences Christopher Marlowe, are rarely performed or studied outside of speciality fields. Why Shakespeare is 'Shakespeare' a byword for literary excellence, and how he earned that reputation not alone, but in collaboration with others.
This spirit of collaboration is echoed for the students in the final assignment which is collaborative group work and presentation.

The three play units provide full teachable units for a Comedy, a History and a Tragedy. These units of work are ready to teach, or they can be used as a template for creating your own unit for another of the plays.

You may be curious about why I chose these plays rather than the more attention grabbing and familiar plays such as Macbeth or Romeo and Juliet. Macbeth, despite its simple story-line contains some of the most diabolically difficult language in Shakespeare, coming as it does from the Jacobean period and the move of the Kings Men to performing in an indoor space in addition to their open air theatre The Globe. Julius Caesar on the other hand come from the middle of Shakespeare's writing career and while also political in nature, its politics are clearer, its plot and language more accessible. It is also the only play without an obvious comic role. Macbeth with themes of power, ambition and time. Added to the supernatural elements requires more explicit and direct instruction. In combination with the language makes this a more difficult play for students to grasp as their introductory play. Julius Caesar also has a political assassination and is about a desire to change the world, even through extreme action. Brutus does not desire power for himself. It is his love of country and patriotism that is used to manipulate him into acting against the head of state. It is a play where reason and argument are used to manipulate the power of the populace for a cause. For students in a 21st century democracy, this approach to power is far easier to recognise.

Why Julius Caesar over Romeo and Juliet? While the great Tragedies all involve at least one suicide. This is one area where we don't want students to romanticise about or relate to closely too. It is more difficult to romantisise to the deaths of middle aged Roman generals who use suicide for cultural reasons, than two teens who do so for 'love'. I have taught students, for whom this consideration is important, and for this reason I would not consider any of the tragedies appropriate. As always use your discretion and professional judgement, you know your class.

If however you want teenagers, or young protagonists with relatable problems, may I suggest Henry IV Part 1. What could a medieval king possibly have to say to a 21st century student? I hear you ask. This is a story of parents and their children, of feeling unable to communicate to a different generation. The spirit of rebellion, the need to mature and accepting the responsibility that comes with that maturity. It also presents some of the greatest comic set pieces and the greatest comic character Shakespeare ever wrote: Falstaff.

Finally, our comedy is The Taming of the Shrew. A play that is very easy to reduce down to a battle of the sexes, but which becomes a more interesting work when viewed through the lens of respectful relationships and personal authenticity. Themes that are relevant to the young adults we teach, as they work out how and who to be in the world.

You might find the approach to these plays a little different to the traditional method of teaching a Shakespearean play. As an alternative to the students stumbling over the language and losing the meaning by sentences stretched to breaking point by halting delivery. I recommend watching the plays with a play script that students can annotate. I recommend this for two reasons, one is simply clarity, professional actors speak these lines far more accurately and with better intonation than even your best reader can. Secondly, a play script is only half a text, the other half of the text is contributed by the performers. By watching the play students gain a much better understanding of how, who and what the characters are speaking and a play script becomes a full text.

To this end I would recommend the best unabridged or as near to unabridged stage productions that you have access to. I have personally found that both the RSC (Royal

Shakespeare Company) and The Globe offer excellent productions and I can recommend both. The RSC production of The Taming of the Shrew, where they switched the genders of the characters, was particularly revelatory when it came to an enhanced understanding of this play.

In the back of this book are the unit program templates with outcomes from the Australian National Curriculum. This can be used as the basis for your own records, or adjusting the outcomes to suit your state or territory and your own execution of the unit.

Shakespeare is the most revered and challenging author that we have the privilege to present to our students. The way that we present this titan of English literature can influence our students perceptions of his works for the rest of their lives. Ask the average person on the street what they think of Shakespeare and you will hear words like 'boring', 'difficult', 'elitist', and 'irrelevant'. Worse still, you may be subject to a tirade that Shakespeare was not the true author of the plays we now attribute to his name. Even more dispiriting than the general rejection of Shakespeare's great works by the general public. Is when you encounter teachers, or indeed whole English faculties, so intimidated by Shakespeare or so insecure about how to teach these texts, that they teach adaptations or abridgements of the plays, reserving the plays themselves for the highest performing students. It would seem Shakespeare is only for the "clever" students and provided that the rest get the basic plot outline, that will suffice.

Shaking up Shakespeare seeks to challenge this. If we believe, that Shakespeare is for everyone, then that is what we must teach: A Shakespeare that is for everyone. As teachers it is important not to allow our own anxieties, or worse regarding Shakespeare to colour our students attitudes. We assume that our students will be frightened approaching the titan of English literature. That his ghost rears before them, like old king Hamlet, filling them with terror. But sad to say, the great Shakespeare film renaissance of the 1990's finished over twenty years ago now. Buried in the mists of time, and as irrelevant to today's students as Laurence Olivier's static camera work and received pronunciation was to my generation. My first Richard III was Ian MacKellen, not Olivier. My Hamlet was Kenneth Branagh. Students today would be more familiar with these actors as Gandalf, and Gilderoy Lockheart not as great Shakespearean actors.

A couple of years ago, I was teaching a history class and while discussing the status of Kabuki theatre in Japanese culture made a reference to Shakespeare as an analogous figure in the western culture. I was met not with understanding nods for the comparison, but the blank stares of 'bunnies in the headlights'. I must have looked at the class incredulously, because one of the boys raised his hand and asked, "Who's Shakespeare?"
They weren't frightened of Shakespeare, they were ignorant of him.
As teachers we can use their ignorance to our advantage. By making Shakespeare exciting and fun.
Let's shake up Shakespeare.

Natalie Muller

How to use this book.

The units of work in this book have been written to run for 30 lessons of 50 min each. If the school you work in has longer or shorter classes, then you will need to make adjustments accordingly.
The units have time built into them specifically for the major assignments to be completed in class. These assignments, form part of the unit and are not an optional extra, but an integral component where the students use the previous 25 lessons worth of learning to complete them.

The programs in this book use the Australian National Curriculum Outcomes for years 8 and 10. They are designed to provide a launching pad for your own program writing, pointing you to the focus of the unit and the lessons that specifically cover each outcome.

Each unit will run as written, and all learning materials, except the films are provided. Full PDF texts of the three plays are available on the Black Cockie Press website free with the code: KBHOHSR034CK www.blackcockiepress.com.au/shop
Alternately, these units can be read and used as a starting off point in designing your own unit of work.

The glossary covers all extracts included in the Year 8 introductory unit. For the full plays I would recommend investing in David Crystal and Ben Crystal's excellent book Shakespeare's words. A glossary and language companion published by Penguin books.

This book has been written with teachers in mind. Whether you are new to teaching needing a helping hand, or an experienced teacher looking for something to reinvigorate your teaching of Shakespeare, you will find this an invaluable resource.

Meet the Upstart Crow

Introducing Shakespeare Year 8 Unit.

Stage: 4 **Topic: Shakespeare?** **Lesson: 1**

Learning Intention: To introduce the concept that Shakespeare is so integrated into our culture that we don't even see him and his work in the influences he has left in our culture.

Teaching strategy: Teacher talk and Student worksheets
Presentation:
- Settle class and roll.
- Assess students existing knowledge by brainstorming Shakespeare on the board as a class. Students may have a very low level of preexisting knowledge.
- Tropes taken from Shakespeare's plays. Ask students where they have seen the following tropes in pop culture:
    - Lovers talking at a balcony. Romeo and Juliet
    - Twins mistaken for each other. Twelfth Night and a Comedy of Errors.
    - A villain with a physical disability. Richard III

- Offer several of the most common idioms and words, if preexisting knowledge is very low start with words first recorded by Shakespeare. Show the students that they quote Shakespeare every day in their speech. Shakespeare is also the first place many common words were recorded i.e. bedroom. In fact he is credited with coining 1500 new words, often by by turning nouns into verbs or creating composite words, like Bed+Room.
- Worksheet on Phrases coined by Shakespeare + Words search.
- Pack up.
Lesson reflection:

Meet The Upstart Crow: Introducing Shakespeare 15

Quote	Phrase	Meaning
if ye should lead her into a fool's paradise, as they say, it were a very gross kind of behaviour, as they say: **Romeo and Juliet**		
Nothing of him that doth fade But doth suffer a sea-change Into something rich and strange. **The Tempest**		
O, beware, my lord, of jealousy; It is the green-eyed monster which doth mock The meat it feeds on; **Othello**		
O gracious lady, Since I received command to do this business I have not slept one wink. **Cymbeline**		
It is more than for some, my lord; it is for all, all I have. He hath eaten me out of house and home; he hath put all my substance into that fat belly of his: **Henry IV part 2**		
I have been in such a pickle since I saw you last **The Tempest**		
The more fool you, for laying on my duty. **The Taming of the Shrew**		
Why then, can one desire too much of a good thing? **As You Like It**		

Quote	Phrase	Meaning
if ye should lead her into **a fool's paradise**, as they say, it were a very gross kind of behaviour, as they say: **Romeo and Juliet**		
Nothing of him that doth fade But doth suffer **a sea-change** Into something rich and strange. **The Tempest**		
O, beware, my lord, of jealousy; It is the **green-eyed monster** which doth mock The meat it feeds on; **Othello**		
O gracious lady, Since I received command to do this business **I have not slept one wink.** **Cymbeline**		
It is more than for some, my lord; it is for all, all I have. He hath eaten me out of house and home; he hath put all my substance into that fat belly of his: **Henry IV part 2**		
I have been in such a pickle since I saw you last **The Tempest**		
The more fool you, for laying on my duty. **The Taming of the Shrew**		
Why then, can one desire **too much of a good thing?** **As You Like It**		

Meet The Upstart Crow: Introducing Shakespeare

```
Z O R Q S B L R S J F A F O L O Y D G J S W V E G J J J V X
E I N R L V X S R S Y U M H M O D O F I D X C V E U Z L D K
L G I S Q U O B R I U S O W G N K W Y J O R R U G E A R Z B
E S R Z S N H K K G E S S L G G X N U L P P B L V Q J B C P
S T A D R Y V M X Y Q U A N N A O S V C E U R N V G U L T K
C X F N I Q X D U N K G I I N V I T A T I O N E O F X E G N
Y D Q P O N A N F H K Y R B N T M A Z O K H W R Y G K M Q A
X X G A K V P O U O F E S L V D H I C V O J F A Z D J P M J
H O V W H J Z A D I E I D O T R I R H M Q R P B S Q F L U E
G H L H O A K M T N R K O O B Y M S P Z I S E L V O O O M E
J D G X P H N R I Q W E N D A K O P T V J A D E D L B Y K Z
T V L I D J O M A A A S H S R O U R F I R V C X A H B M R L
C Z B N K M O U T H E D K T E B A J M D N A K T E L L E R O
V Q S A A D X W O P F C D A F C N I T M S G N O A T N N Q W
K V T Y Z A J V L J C K A I A J W H E U X E U N T Z L T W C
I N R Y C R A E U I F H Y N C X N F J K M R S I K X S C V G
V Y Q Q U A R R E L S O M E E T D D M U L J W V S Q M S X I
S B G F B R Z F X J H J I D D T I A N M I E P L V H R H S K
B R X V K C G A N M I Z I R M A E O E G Q C B G V T A C Q K
R A B W G B A R E O E V P C Q B M J N T W Z E T D M D B K R
K Q R D F X U F A I N V U L N E R A B L E L G D Z R G H L Y
R N Y W J R N K X B X D W O H E X Q J F V U K J N Z R K Q E
O Q K J C P R U M Z G R O W N E O I S E C P G G D A Q I T G
I I L L W P D N H R E M O R S E L E S S S S M S B C X A N Z
H L B U F S C X C H C H V Q T P H V F O R T U N E K B A Q E
V F J L X B P P F G T E S Z A N Y F U H Y A I B D P G O I O
N V S Q T L H N Y S U C C E S S F U L M I I D C R Q W L T V
A I M C V O R Y N A W I H L U C W U L G R R N T O H I D I S
I G V P P K M I U F F C V M S H O B R F K S L E O M R F G K
E Y A N S E E J M H V J Y P J F A I R Y L A N D M A Q P W A
```

ADDICTION
BAREFACED
BEDROOM
BLOODSTAINED
CHEAP
DOMINEERING
DOWNSTAIRS
EMPLOYMENT
FAIRYLAND
FORTUNE
FOUL
FULL
GROWN
INDISTINGUISHABLE
INVITATION
INVULNERABLE
JADED
JUICED
MAJESTIC
MONUMENTAL
MOONBEAM
MORTIFYING
MOUTHED
QUARRELSOME
REMORSELESS
SAVAGE
SUCCESSFUL
TELLER
UPSTAIRS
VULNERABLE
ZANY

Stage: 4   Topic: Is Shakespeare for everyone   Lesson: 2

Learning Intention: Overcome any hesitancy about treating Shakespeare as just another text. Help students understand that these plays, while old are still texts just like any other they encounter. Once you have an "in" they are able to be understood, no differently than a book, game or film.

Teaching strategy: Through the use of Teacher centred learning and Multi Media resources and classroom discussion.

Presentation:

- Settle class and Roll.
- Talk about things that they do that need to be learnt and initiated into to understand and get the most out of: card games, sport, learning an instrument etc. Ask the student who got them into this interest? Why was it so important to them that they took the time to learn it?

Explain to them that Shakespeare's plays are a bit like these interests, that you need certain skills and knowledge to get the most out of them.

- Show 10 min max clip of your choice. No explanation, no context, just actors and language. Use a full text version not a dumbed down version. The Globe and the RSC have some good clips, I have a breakdown of two clips in the teachers notes following if you don't feel confident breaking down a clip yourself.
- Ask the students what they did and did not understand.
- Re-watch the clip. This time breaking it down so that the characters and the context are intelligible to the students.
- Pack up

Lesson reflection:

Scene Breakdown Royal Shakespeare Company
Antony and Cleopatra Act 1 Scene 3

SCENE III. The same. Another room.

Enter CLEOPATRA, CHARMIAN, IRAS, and ALEXAS

CLEOPATRA: Where is he?

CHARMIAN: I did not see him since.

(Antony has been called away by a messenger from Rome and Cleopatra wants to know what is going on.)

CLEOPATRA: See where he is, who's with him, what he does:

I did not send you: if you find him sad,

Say I am dancing; if in mirth, report

That I am sudden sick: quick, and return.

Exit ALEXAS

(Cleopatra sends a servant to find Antony and to inform him of a contrary disposition to whatever the servant finds him in.)

CHARMIAN: Madam, methinks, if you did love him dearly,

You do not hold the method to enforce

The like from him.

(Charmian, the queens confidant, thinks her mistresses instructions are likely to lose her Antony's affection.)

CLEOPATRA: What should I do, I do not?

CHARMIAN: In each thing give him way, cross him nothing.

CLEOPATRA: Thou teachest like a fool; the way to lose him.

Cleopatra argues that bering compliant and submissive will lose Antony's affection.

CHARMIAN: Tempt him not so too far; I wish, forbear:

In time we hate that which we often fear.

(Charmian cautions that you can only push men so far.)

But here comes Antony.

Enter MARK ANTONY

CLEOPATRA: I am sick and sullen.

(Antony obviously enters happy, so Cleopatra will pretend to be sick.)

MARK ANTONY: I am sorry to give breathing to my purpose,--

CLEOPATRA: Help me away, dear Charmian; I shall fall:

It cannot be thus long, the sides of nature

Will not sustain it.

(Cleopatra continues playacting as Antony tries to tell the news that has made him happy.)

MARK ANTONY: Now, my dearest queen,--

CLEOPATRA: Pray you, stand further from me.

MARK ANTONY: What's the matter?

(Antony finally realises that Cleopatra is annoyed with his mood.)

CLEOPATRA: I know, by that same eye, there's some good news.

What says the married woman? You may go:

Would she had never given you leave to come!

Let her not say 'tis I that keep you here:

I have no power upon you; hers you are.

(Cleopatra thinks the message relates to Antony's Roman wife and is jealous.)

MARK ANTONY: The gods best know,--

CLEOPATRA: O, never was there queen

So mightily betray'd! yet at the first

I saw the treasons planted.

(She is worried about her position and his support.)

MARK ANTONY: Cleopatra,--

CLEOPATRA: Why should I think you can be mine and true,

Though you in swearing shake the throned gods,

Who have been false to Fulvia? Riotous madness,

To be entangled with those mouth-made vows,

Which break themselves in swearing!

(Now Cleopatra is having fun playing the betrayed lover.)

MARK ANTONY: Most sweet queen,--

CLEOPATRA: Nay, pray you, seek no colour for your going,

But bid farewell, and go: when you sued staying,

Then was the time for words: no going then;

Eternity was in our lips and eyes,

Bliss in our brows' bent; none our parts so poor,

But was a race of heaven: they are so still,

Or thou, the greatest soldier of the world,

Art turn'd the greatest liar.

(She is still playing with him, continually interrupting his efforts to explain himself.)

MARK ANTONY: How now, lady!

CLEOPATRA: I would I had thy inches; thou shouldst know

There were a heart in Egypt.

MARK ANTONY: Hear me, queen:

The strong necessity of time commands

Our services awhile; but my full heart

Remains in use with you.

(Antony finally asserts himself. He is one of the most powerful men in Rome, he will be heard, respectfully he is recalled to Rome, but his full allegiance and love shall remain behind with her.)

Scene Breakdown Royal Shakespeare Company
As You Like It Act III Scene 2

(Orlando is in love with Rosalind, but has been forced to flee to the Forest Arden. Rosalind is on love with Orlando. She has been banished from the court and also has fled with her cousin Celia to the forest. Rosalind is currently disguised as a boy called Ganymede. Orlando doesn't know that Rosalind is Ganymede. Orlando had trouble speaking to Rosalind, but he has no trouble talking with Ganymede a boy of his own age.)

ROSALIND: No; I will not cast away my physic but on those that are sick. There is a man haunts the forest, that abuses our young plants with carving 'Rosalind' on their barks; hangs odes upon hawthorns, and elegies on brambles; all, forsooth, deifying the name of Rosalind. If I could meet that fancy-monger, I would give him some good counsel, for he seems to have the quotidian of love upon him.

There is someone in the forest who is defacing the trees with poetry to Rosalind, if she were to meet him, she would know how to counsel him out of this love he swears by.

ORLANDO: I am he that is so love-shak'd, I pray you tell me your remedy.

ROSALIND: There is none of my uncle's marks upon you. He taught me how to know a man in love; in which cage of rushes I am sure you are not prisoner.
(Rosalind doesn't believe that he really is in love because he doesn't fit the image of romantic stereotypes.)

ORLANDO: What were his marks?

ROSALIND: A lean cheek, which you have not; a blue eye and sunken, which you have not; an unquestionable spirit, which you have not; a beard neglected, which you have not (but I pardon you for that, for simply your having in beard is a younger brother's revenue); then your hose should be ungarter'd, your bonnet unbanded, your sleeve unbutton'd, your shoe untied, and every thing about you demonstrating a careless desolation. But you are no such man; you are rather point-device in your accoustrements, as loving yourself, than seeming the lover of any other.

ORLANDO:Fair youth, I would I could make thee believe I love.
(Orlando is adamant he is actually in love.)

ROSALIND: Me believe it? You may as soon make her that you love believe it, which I warrant she is apter to do than to confess she does. That is one of the points in the which women still give the lie to their consciences. But in good sooth, are you he that hangs the verses on the trees, wherein Rosalind is so admir'd?
(Rosalind says that saying you are in love is no good, you have to be able to make you beloved believe that you love her.)

ORLANDO: I swear to thee, youth, by the white hand of Rosalind, I am that he, that unfortunate he.

ROSALIND: But are you so much in love as your rhymes speak?

ORLANDO: Neither rhyme nor reason can express how much.

ROSALIND: Love is merely a madness, and I tell you, deserves as well a dark house and a whip as madmen do; and the reason why they are not so punish'd and cur'd is, that the lunacy is so ordinary that the whippers are in love too. Yet I profess curing it by counsel.

(Rosalind is adamant that love is just a madness, which is so widespread that it is not seen as such and it can be cured by counsel.)

ORLANDO: Did you ever cure any so?

ROSALIND: Yes, one, and in this manner. He was to imagine me his love, his mistress; and I set him every day to woo me. At which time would I, being but a moonish youth, grieve, be effeminate, changeable, longing and liking, proud, fantastical, apish, shallow, inconstant, full of tears, full of smiles; for every passion something, and for no passion truly any thing, as boys and women are for the most part cattle of this colour; would now like him, now loathe him; then entertain him, then forswear him; now weep for him, then spit at him; that I drave my suitor from his mad humor of love to a living humor of madness, which was, to forswear the full stream of the world, and to live in a nook merely monastic. And thus I cur'd him, and this way will I take upon me to wash your liver as clean as a sound sheep's heart, that there shall not be one spot of love in't.

(Rosalind claims to have cured one of love by putting it to the test, by behaving as a real human being with real human emotions, bad moods, changeability and proving that to actually love another person is a lot harder than loving an idealised image, which is what Orlando is currently doing.)

ORLANDO: I would not be cur'd, youth.

(Orlando claims to be truly in love and will not be cured in this way.)

ROSALIND: I would cure you, if you would but call me Rosalind, and come every day to my cote and woo me.

(Rosalind will have Orlando court her, while she continues to pretend to be the boy Ganymede.)

ORLANDO: Now, by the faith of my love, I will. Tell me where it is.

ROSALIND: Go with me to it, and I'll show it you; and by the way, you shall tell me where in the forest you live. Will you go?

ORLANDO: With all my heart, good youth.

ROSALIND: Nay, you must call me Rosalind. Come, sister, will you go?

(Orlando agrees to this arrangement and Rosalind shows him where 'he' and his 'sister' live.)

Stage: 4   Topic: How has Shakespeare changed over time?   Lesson: 3

Learning Intention: Explain that Shakespeare has become more intimidating over time and that they way audiences respond to the texts has changed over 400 years.

Teaching strategy: Teacher led class notes.
Presentation:
- Settle class and Roll.
- Either copying or dictated notes or comprehension passage, depending on your assessment of the classes ability and behaviour. However a class with very poor literacy levels and poor behaviour can actually benefit from copying notes off the board. Read the notes to them first and discuss any questions that they have before they start copying them.
The comprehension passages are fine as independent work for a top class, as they will cope with the independent reading, and it can be a chance to train them to answer questions in full sentences. However, should you wish to use it with a well behaved, but lower ability class, reading passages aloud around the class and answering the questions together on the board also works well.
- If the class has been given the passage as independent reading go over the answers with the class.
- Pack up.
Lesson reflection:

How has Shakespeare changed over time?

During his lifetime Shakespeare was arguably one of the most, if not the most, popular and respected playwrights working in the late Elizabethan and early Jacobean theatre scene. No other playwright from this period had their complete works collected and anthologised by their colleagues after their deaths. The first folio, is both a memorial and a business venture, there was clearly a market for Shakespeare's works in the years after his death, for it to be worth a publisher's expense in producing such a work. Ben Johnson, a friend and rival playwright to Shakespeare, offered a dedicatory poem to this volume in which he said:
Thou art a monument without a tomb,
And art alive still while thy book doth live
And we have wits to read and praise to give.

After the fire of 1613 that destroyed the original Globe theatre, it was rebuilt on the same site by the Kings Men, and Shakespeare's works continued to be part of their repertoire. This theatre and London's active theatre scene stopped abruptly, when a parliamentary ordinance on September 6 1642 closed the theatres. Theatre would not return to England until after the restoration of the Monarchy in 1660 when Charles II lifted the ban. However, theatrical taste had shifted in the nearly two decades of civil wars and Interregnum or the period of the Puritan led republic. Shakespeare was no longer the most fashionable of playwrights and his plays would be less performed and radically transformed to meet the requirements of restoration tastes.

By the mid 18th century, a Shakespeare revival led by star actor David Garrick, would see his plays command a quarter of all theatre performances. His works would also start to be translated into other European languages as he became better known on the continent. This also led to an interest in the biography of the author and a search, for what became the literary holy grail, manuscript copies of Shakespeare's works. Forgeries proliferated as people sought a tangible physical link to Shakespeare.

By the late 18th and early 19th centuries, the Romantic poets, especially Coleridge and Keats had helped to propagate the notion of Shakespeare as a naturalistic, lone genius, whom they identified with. This would lead to the deification (making a god) of Shakespeare as the finest writer of all time who could not be surpassed. Theatrical performances also became far more elaborate, with huge sets, that required all action stop to change them. The traditional way of speaking Shakespeare, using strict iambic pentameter, ignoring the actual rhythms of the lines would continue. However most people encountered Shakespeare not in performance, but by reading his works.

The 20th century, sees Shakespeare's plays make their way to cinema. Silent film adaptations of Shakespeare's plays date back to the 1900's. For the Mid 20th century Shakespeare on film would be popularised by the films of the English Sir Lawrence Olivier and the American film maker Orson Wells. Olivier would bring a "traditional" stage aesthetic to his performances. While Orson Wells would bring a more naturalistic mode of performance to the plays. As of 2020 there are 1500 known films and adaptations of Shakespeare's plays from across the globe. Theatre performances would also radically change during this period, stripping back the elaborate sets and increasingly allowing the language and performance to stand on its own, as it had done when the plays were written.

The 21st century has seen a radical shift in the way Shakespeare is thought of. Modern scholarship has shown a Shakespeare who was not a lone genius, of godlike qualities, but a man who competed with and collaborated with other playwrights. Who wrote for the popular stage and popular actors, fitting parts to their talents and to stretch them and their capabilities. A man who managed to negotiate a tricky social and political climate. A period of upheavals and shifts and concerns, that are reflected in the plays he produced for London audiences. This is the man and the works we will be studying.

Questions.

1. What evidence do we have that Shakespeare was well respected in his own time?
2. What political events after Shakespeare's death left his plays less performed?
3. Who was the actor who saw a Shakespeare revival in the 18th century?
4. During the 19th century, how did most people engage with Shakespeare's plays?
5. What new medium did Shakespeare's plays migrate to in the 20th century?
6. How many different film adaptations of Shakespeare's plays are known to exist?
7. How has modern scholarship changed our understanding of Shakespeare in the 21st century?

Stage: 4 **Topic: Shakespeare's Background** **Lesson: 4**

Learning Intention: Understand Shakespeare was an ordinary man who wrote plays. Where he came from and who his family was.

Teaching strategy: Class notes and worksheets

Presentation:
- Settle class and Roll
- Explain that Shakespeare was an ordinary man for much of his life, especially his early life and so there are big gaps in what we know of his life outside his works because people did not leave much of a paper trail if they were not very rich and politically powerful. Timeline of Shakespeare's life. Either hand out or copy off board.
- Introduction to Elizabethan Theatre and travelling companies Comprehension passage or Notes.
- Letter home from London – Why I left!

Students to write a letter from Shakespeare home to Stratford explaining to his wife, parents and children why he felt the need to leave home for London.

- Pack up.

Lesson reflection:

Shakespeare Timeline

23rd April 1564 born Stratford-upon-Avon
1582 The Lord Chamberlain's men become active.
28th November 1582 marriage licence issued for William Shakespeare and Anne Hathaway.
26th May 1583 Baptism of William and Anne's daughter Susanna.
2nd February 1585 Baptism of William and Anne's twins Hamnet and Judith.
1586 Shakespeare leaves Stratford.
1592 Robert Greene refers to Shakespeare as an 'upstart crow' in his A Groats Worth of Wit
August 1592- January 1593 Plague in London closes the theatres. Shakespeare turns to poetry writing supported by the patronage of The Earl of Southampton.
1593 Publishes Venus and Adonis and in 1594 Publishes Lucrece, both through a former school mate now publisher Richard Field.
1593 Christopher Marlowe murdered.
1594 The Chamberlains Men are founded by Richard Burbage
15th March 1595 Shakespeare named as a sharer in The Chamberlains Men
1597 The Isle of Dogs scandal sees Ben Jonson imprisoned and the Swan Theatre closed to playing.
December 1598 The tenancy on the land that The Theatre stood on expires. The Chamberlains Men demolish their old Theatre and remove the timber to their newly leased site on the Southbank.
Spring 1599 Work begins of the Chamberlains men's new Theatre The Globe.
1599 William Kemp leaves The Chamberlains Men and Robert Armin joins them as their new clown. Shakespeare will write different types of Comic characters for their new commedian.
1st June 1599 'The Bishops Ban' bans the production of English History plays, ending Shakespeare's great cycle of plays from Richard II to Richard III.
Feb 1601 The Chamberlains Men paid to perform Richard II by the Earl of Essex before his failed coup. They are called in by the authorities to explain themselves, but escape censure.
1603 Queen Elizabeth I dies
19th March 1603 The Lord Chamberlain dies leaving the company without a patron.
19th May 1603 the former Chamberlain's Men gain a new patron in King James I, becoming The Kings Men.
Late July 1606 – mid-November 1606 Theatres closed due to the plague in London. The Kings Men and other London companies tour the provinces.
1608 The Kings Men reacquire the lease of The Blackfriars Theatre, giving them an indoor performance venue with a more sophisticated audience.
1611 Shakespeare write his final solo play The Tempest.
1613 The Globe theatre burns down due to an accident during a performance of Henry VIII, a collaboration between Shakespeare and Fletcher. Shakespeare retires to Stratford-upon-Avon.
23rd April 1616 Shakespeare dies.
1623 The first folio, the first complete collection of Shakespeare's plays is published by his former colleagues.

Elizabethan theatre and travelling companies.

In 1576 two permanent theatres were erected The Red Lion which quickly disappeared and The Theatre built by John Brayne and James Burbage. Until this point all players had been travelling companies. Companies of actors who take their performances across the country, setting up in towns and performing for a set amount of time before moving on. These companies would have had small repertoires of plays that they knew well and took with them from town to town. Playwrights were not such an important feature of this type of theatre. The permanent theatres would change that.

Since the audience of a permanent theatre was more fixed than the ever changing one of the travelling troupe, theatre companies had to vary their offerings to appeal to returning audiences. The Admirals men, a rival company to The Chamberlain's Men, performed 38 plays in the during the playing season of 1593/95. To feed this hunger for novelty, the professional playwright was born.

Elizabethan theatres and theatre companies operated within a legal fiction, that was, that performances of plays were permitted as a 'dress rehearsal' for court performances. This left theatre companies vulnerable to the whims of their monarch, who could close them down at a moment's notice. Another problem facing Theatre companies was the loss of their patron, as happened to The Chamberlain's Men when the Lord Chamberlain died. Fortunately, they found a new patron in their new monarch, becoming the Kings Men.

With the rise of the permanent theatre, travelling companies did not die out, but continued, being a breeding ground for new talent. As well as a way for London companies to make money, when London performance was not possible, such as over summer when theatres closed or when Plague closed the theatres. Touring companies would play towns and cities, as well as private performances in courtiers households. However, life on the road was not easy, especially as rising puritanical attitudes closed towns to performance. Stratford-upon-Avon was one such town, in spite of theatre making Shakespeare one of its wealthiest citizens, authorities increasingly discouraged playing in the town.

- When was the first permanent theatre built in London?
- Why did the new theatres need more plays?
- How did the theatres satisfy the appetite for novelty in their audiences?
- What was the legal fiction that allowed playing to become a permanent fixture in London?
- Why did travelling playing continue even with the permanent theatres?

Stage: 4 **Topic: The Elizabethan Theatre** **Lesson: 5**

Learning Intention: To understand who were involved in the producing of a play in Elizabethan London and who were the enemies of the Theatre.

Teaching strategy: Student centred work.

Presentation:

- Settle class and Roll.
- Who is who of Elizabethan Theatre. Worksheet Mix and Match the titles with the descriptions.
- Go through Sheet with students and discuss who are friends of the Theatre and who are its enemies and why?
- Draw up a table on the board and divide the list into friends and enemies giving reasons why each ended up where they did. More advanced students can do this activity on their own after discussion.
- Pack up

Lesson reflection:

Who's who of Elizabethan Theatre	
Audiences	Members of a religious reform moment that sought to 'purify' the Church of England of remaining Roman Catholic practices. The term 'puritan' was a pejorative term even in Shakespeare's time, and was seen as a byword for eliminating all sources of pleasure, including The Theatre.
Puritans	A noble and aristocratic person who could obtain a licence for a Theatre company allowing them to perform. This protection and patronage was reflected in the name of the company. Eg, The Lord Chamberlain's Men were named because The Lord Chamberlain was their patron.
Actors	This refers to the official state church: The Church of England, headed by the Monarch and able to wield significant influence over the society as a whole.
Companies	The Master of Revels was the official state censor, he dictated what could and could not be said on stage, or in printed texts.
Patrons	The assembled spectators of a public event, such as play, concert, sporting event etc.
Playwrights	Professionals whose job it is to perform in plays.
The Censor	Groups of professional actors, managers, playwrights and other theatre professionals who produce plays for the public.
The Church	Professionals whose job it is to compose plays.

Stage: 4   **Topic: Life cycle of a play**   **Lesson: 6**

Learning Intention: What was the life cycle of a play in the Elizabethan theatre?

Teaching strategy: Class notes/close passage and individual creative work i.e. letter home or cartoon strip.

Presentation:

- Settle class and Roll
- Daily life in the theatre notes. Read through together or have students read through silently.
- Write a letter home to Stratford-upon-Avon detailing your life in the theatre. How is your training going? How are you finding people to teach you the craft of writing?
- or
- Create a cartoon detailing the life cycle of a play from idea to performance.
- Pack up

Lesson reflection:

Daily life in the theatre.

What was the process followed by theatre companies to get a play onto the stage?

The Pitch: Theatre companies were always commissioning new plays to feed their theatres. Plays sold for approx £6 each. Companies could pay hundreds of pounds per year for new plays. New plays were the engine that drove audiences to the theatre. Playwrights or groups of playwrights, up to five writers working collaboratively, would pitch story ideas to the actor sharers of a theatre. A reliable playwright who could produce high quality plays was valuable to a theatre and managers often tried to bind writers to themselves exclusively. This was not really possible, unless like Shakespeare the playwright had a monetary interest in the theatre company they wrote for. The Sharers would then decide which plays they wanted to accept, and the playwright or group of playwrights would then be loaned an advance payment and write the play to the theatre's deadline.

Before Rehearsals: Once a play was delivered to a theatre company, it would be read through by the actor sharers who would decide whether they wanted to stage the play. Once they decided they would stage the play the actors would be given their own individual parts. The complete play would be kept by the 'book-keeper' a role akin to a modern day prompter and stage manager. He would also be responsible for making the copies that the actors learn their lines from.
Actors would be then given their parts, not the whole play to learn. This was achieved by giving each actor the last few words of preceding dialogue so that they knew their cues.

The Master of Revels: Before a play could be staged it had to be approved by the official censor called the Master of Revels. He would give approval for a play to be performed, or dictate what changes needed to be made to allow for performance. These changes would usually be made by the 'book-keeper'.

Rehearsals: These were held in the morning before the afternoon performance. Actors would be given their costumes and the props that they would be using. Sword fights would be choreographed, and practised. The costumes were often exceedingly valuable, contemporary and reflected character types, thus Kings and Queens all wore certain costumes to identify them by their title. Caesar for instance would not have worn a toga, but would have been dressed more like an Elizabethan nobleman. Because there were laws forbidding commoners to wear the clothes of the nobility, theatres had special permission to use expensive clothes. They often bought them from servants who were willed them by masters, or had them commissioned specially. Theatres could spend as much as £300 on costumes per year. Boys and hired actors would know nothing of the play they were in beyond their own part, so rehearsals were their first experience of the full play.

Performance: Performances of plays took place between 2pm and 5pm before it was too dark for the audience to return home. A play may be performed several times in the course of a year and may even enter the repertoire of the company and remain popular for years. If a play was not well received it may receive only a single performance before being dropped. The Admirals Men, of whom good records remain, played 14 play in one month, 6 of which received only one performance before being dropped.

Afterlife: The afterlife of a play was very varied. Some, continued to be performed for many years, others fell out of favour quickly. Others were published in quatros or octavos, small books, by the playhouse for the growing reading public. In Shakespeare's lifetime 17 or nearly half of the 36 plays he wrote were published in this way.

Stage: 4   Topic: Upstart Crow – Shakespeare appears!   Lesson: 7

Learning Intention: to look at the first appearance of Shakespeare in print after his departure for London.

Teaching strategy: Teacher directed and Student centred work.

Presentation:

- Settle class and Roll.
- Introduce Robert Greene – use teachers notes
- Read attached passage from Robert Greene's A Groats Worth of Wit to the students. Ask them what they don't understand? And what they think it means?
- Students do questions on the Upstart Crow worksheet, either independently or as a class depending on ability.
- Pack up

Lesson reflection:

Robert Greene:

Born in 1558 six years earlier than Shakespeare, in Norwich, Robert Green was a writer and playwright whom we now identify as one of the University Wits. He studied at both Oxford and Cambridge, receiving a Master of Arts from both universities. A thing he was very proud of and put on the title page of his publications. He was the author of four solo plays, one co-written play and a large number of romances and pamphlets. He died at 35 in 1592. He is chiefly remembered for his pamphlet published in 1592 Groats-worth of Wit bought with a Million or repentance. In which we find the first textual reference to Shakespeare as a playwright in London.

Base minded men all three of you, if by my misery ye be not warned: for unto none of you (like me) sought those burrs to cleave: those Puppets (I mean) that speak from our mouths, those Antics garnished in our colours. Is it not strange that I, to whom they all have been beholding: is it not like that you, to whom they all have been beholding, shall (were ye in that case that I am now) be both at once of them forsaken? Yes, trust them not: for there is an upstart Crow, beautified with our feathers, that with his Tygers heart wrapped in a Players hide, supposes he is as well able to bombast out a blank verse as the best of you: and being an absolute Johannes factotum, is in his own conceit the only Shake-scene in a country. O that I might entreat your rare wits to be employed in more profitable courses: and let those Apes imitate your past excellence, and never more acquaint them with your admired inventions. I know the best husband of you all will never prove an Usurer, and the kindest of them all will never seek you a kind nurse: yet while you may, seek you better Masters; for it is pity men of such rare wits, should be subject to the pleasure of such rude grooms.

Base minded men all three of you, if by my misery ye be not warned:
(Take me as your warning gentlemen)
for unto none of you (like me) sought those burrs to cleave: those Puppets (I mean) that speak from our mouths, those Antics garnished in our colours.
(You have not tried to detach these playwrights who imitate us, the university trained writers, to our detriment.)
Is it not strange that I, to whom they all have been beholding: is it not like that you, to whom they all have been beholding, shall (were ye in that case that I am now) be both at once of them forsaken?
(These playwrights who have been looking up to us are not going to do so for long and are likely to abandon you, as they have done to me.)
Yes, trust them not: for there is an upstart Crow, beautified with our feathers, that with his Tygers heart wrapped in a Players hide, supposes he is as well able to bombast out a blank verse as the best of you: and being an absolute Johannes factotum, is in his own conceit the only Shake-scene in a country.
(Chief amongst these imitators is a crow who is using our language, our techniques to make himself more beautiful. This is a reference to the story attributed to Aesop and later Phaderus, where a crow finding peacock feathers wears them to look more beautiful and has them stripped from him by the other birds. This deceptively tame creature, is actually a tiger who thinks because he can imitate us in blank verse he is as good as us. That his belief that he can turn his hand at anything makes him the best.)
O that I might entreat your rare wits to be employed in more profitable courses: and let

those Apes imitate your past excellence, and never more acquaint them with your admired inventions.

(Us university men need to stick together and should not collaborate outside our circle, we should certainly not share our innovations in technique with theses newcomers.)

I know the best husband of you all will never prove an Usurer, and the kindest of them all will never seek you a kind nurse: yet while you may, seek you better Masters; for it is pity men of such rare wits, should be subject to the pleasure of such rude grooms.

(I know none of you would lend out your skills to people beneath you, nor allow them to think you would help them. I know you would only seek out collaboration with our sort of writers and higher. And that it is a shame that less educated men are mocking and using us.)

Questions:

- What does this tell us about the type of men the author thinks should be writing?
- Who does the author think are threatening the university trained writers?
- What does the author think of the writer he calls an upstart Crow?
- "Tygers heart wrapped in a Players hide" is a misquote from Shakespeare's Henry VI Part 3 "oh tigers heart wrapped in woman's hide!" What does the author fear that this young writer will do to writers like himself?
- What warning does the author give to his fellow university trained writers at the end of the passage?
- What do you think this is telling us about the changing landscape amongst playwrights in London at this time? Who is not happy about it?
- What does this imply about how Shakespeare was seen by his contemporaries in this early part of his career?

Stage: 4   Topic: Not a lone Genius, but one of many   Lesson: 8 and 9

Learning Intention: To understand that Shakespeare was not a lone genius, but one of many playwrights who worked in London.

Teaching strategy: Teacher directed and student centred learning.
Presentation:
- Settle class and Roll.
- Notes: How to become a playwright. University trained men Vs Theatre trained men.
- Collaborative writing – Shakespeare as both mentor and student.
- Collaborative writing activity. Divide the class into three groups. Each group is given one act of the Goldilocks and the three bears. Only give students their own act, do not give them the whole synopsis. Students write the play script for their act of the play. Then have the Act 1 writers join up with an Act 2 and an Act 3 writer and read their now complete scripts to the class.
Discuss with the class how they found this process and what they thought of the results.
- Pack up
Lesson reflection:

How to become a playwright.

Play writing, as we have seen, could be a very lucrative profession for a talented and educated young man. But how did an aspiring writer actually break into the profession? Two avenues were open to the aspiring playwright. University educated playwrights like Christopher Marlowe, Robert Greene, Thomas Peele, were able to pursue play writing as a profession due to their education and their superior financial and social status as gentlemen. University educated men would have honed their craft writing for and performing in university productions, before launching themselves in a professional arena

For writers like Shakespeare, Kyd and Jonson, who came form more humble backgrounds the path to becoming a playwright was less direct. Becoming an actor as a way to familiarise oneself with the conventions of the theatre, seems to have been a common stepping stone for writers like Shakespeare and Jonson, both of whom were actors. Shakespeare continuing acting for most of his career, performing in plays for The Chamberlain's Men. Jonson appears to have stopped acting once he had become successful as a freelance playwright. For writers wishing to learn and develop their craft outside the university context, it appears that making a name with a solo project was vital. Shakespeare's first two plays are solo comedies, The Taming of the Shrew and Two Gentlemen of Verona. Jonson too appears to have produced solo plays before attracting the attention of a more established writer to collaborate with.

Co-writing must have offered attractions to both parties, the more inexperienced writer, gaining experience in writing in an unfamiliar form. In Shakespeare's case learning to write history plays with Nashe and Marlowe and tragedy with Peele. For the more established playwright, the younger co-writer would offer new ideas keeping the work fashionable and relevant. It also offered the possibility of the senior writer taking on more commissions by farming the work out in pieces to writers who are eager to prove themselves.

So how did co-writing work?
The writers worked from a basic story line, and they would be assigned parts of the play to produce. Shakespeare is believed to have contributed only 20% of the lines in Henry VI Part I while in his collaboration with Peele on Titus Andronicus Shakespeare is believed to have written acts 3-5 while Peele wrote the opening acts 1 and 2. At the end of his career Shakespeare was the more experienced playwright in his collaborations with Middleton on Timon of Athens. With Wilkins on Pericles and with Fletcher on Henry VIII and The Two Noble Kinsmen.

Co-writing outline.

Goldilocks and the Three Bears as an Elizabethan Revenge Tragedy

Act 1 Scene 1: Mama Pear and Papa Bear are sitting down to breakfast. Mama Bear talks of the robberies that have been plaguing the village on the edge of their wood. Papa Bear reassures Mama Bear that their home deep in the wood is safe from any robbers. Besides no one but the most stupid or evil person would dare attack their home. They decide to go for a walk to catch some breakfast, leaving Baby Bear asleep in bed.

Act 2 Scene 1: Goldilocks, the notorious thief, comes across the empty house. She gives a speech about how she will rob the house and kill anyone she finds inside.

Act 2 Scene 2: The bears return from their hunt to find the house broken into. Goldilocks appears at the window with the bloody covers from Baby Bears bed, and threatens them if they do not let her leave safely. Mama Bear laments Baby Bear.

Act 3 Scene 1: Inside the Bears house Goldilocks is packing away her booty, she is congratulating herself on having robbed the bears who are the most powerful people in the woods, she now feels invincible.

Act 3 Scene 2: Papa Bear reassures Mama Bear that this insult will not pass by, he will have revenge. As Goldilocks emerges from the house Papa Bear fights her and they exit off stage with Mama Bear relaying how her husband has killed Goldilocks. Pappa Bear returns to the stage with their stolen things, and reveals that Goldilocks managed to wound him badly. He collapses and dies and Mama Bear laments.

Stage: 4   **Topic: Dangers of writing**   **Lesson: 10**

Learning Intention: To understand the volatile nature of Elizabethan Theatre.

Teaching strategy: Teacher directed learning and Student centred learning.

Presentation:
- Settle class and Roll.
- Pitfalls of theatre life. Worksheet read through and discuss.
- How did Shakespeare and his company cope with these?
- Whose Who of the Elizabethan stage worksheet.
- Who weren't so lucky? What happened to them?
- Wanted posters
- Pack up

Lesson reflection:

Pitfalls of theatre life.

During the Elizabethan period, actor was not a legal profession and actors could be subject to Tudor Poor Laws as 'vagrants' or 'rogues' and subject to legal penalties, including whipping or even death. To be able to act legally, actors would join together and form companies under the protection of a nobleman, with a title of Baron or Higher. Acting companies were fluid and broke up or changed members frequently. Part of what makes The Lord Chamberlain's/King's men remarkable is their longevity. Because acting was not a recognised profession many actors that we know of today, also served apprenticeships in other trades, playwright and actor Benjamin Jonson was a bricklayer and a soldier, while comedian Robert Armin was a goldsmith.

Obstacles that befell Playing companies and made theatrical life precarious were numerous.

Rain: Theatres were open air structures and plays were performed in the afternoon, between 2pm and ending before sundown. In the event of bad weather, audiences standing in the yard would get wet. Depending on the theatre the actors may also get wet. The Globe which was specially built by and for The Chamberlain's/King's Men, had a canopy over the stage to protect them from rain.

Fire or Collapse: Wood and thatch buildings could and did catch fire. In 1613 during a performance of Shakespeare and Fletcher's play Henry VIII, The Globe caught fire. Shoddy construction and overcrowding was also a danger. In August 1599 a house where a puppet theatre was being performed collapsed, killing 5 spectators and injuring 30-40 more. And in 1583 the gallery of a bear baiting ring collapsed killing 8 spectators.

Neighbour complaints: Theatre audiences are loud and the increasingly puritanical attitudes that developed during this period, led to the banning of playing within the city limits. Theatres were therefore constructed outside the city limits, starting with Shorditch on the city's north eastern border, before shifting to the Southbank of the Themes, which even today is an entertainment district of London. Theatres were also criticised for the practice of boys and men cross dressing to play female parts, which religious fundamentalists saw as immoral.

Plague: Outbreaks of Plague in London caused the closure of theatres for prolonged periods of time. Plague deaths rising to above thirty a week caused the automatic closure of all theatres by order of the Privy Council.

Offending the powerful: Offending the powerful was a dangerous proposition. The satirical play The Isle of Dogs, saw its authors Ben Jonson and Thomas Nashe imprisoned and the Swan Theatre closed to playing for about a year. Ben Jonson again offended the powerful, with his Eastward Ho, to which King James I took offence. Though this did not spill over to harm other theatre companies, as the Isle of Dogs scandal had. Shakespeare had a brush with offending the powerful with his comic character Falstaff, originally named Oldfield. A descendant of an early protestant martyr also called Oldfield took offence at his ancestor's name being associated with the drunken rogue. Shakespeare avoided problems by renaming his character. Official edicts also caused problems, such as the 1599 Bishops ban, which put an end to the

English history plays which had been incredibly popular. And the act of parliament of May 1606 which banned swearing from the public stage, punished by a ten pound Fine. This required the rewriting of passages to remove the offending words from all plays in the company's repertoire.

Whose who of the Elizabethan Stage?

Robert Greene - 1558 – 1592. One of the old guard of Elizabethan playwrights. A University Wit, he was proud of having a Master of arts from both universities, Oxford and Cambridge. Famous for his glancing reference to Shakespeare in his posthumously published: A groats worth of wit.

George Peele - July 1556 – buried 9 November 1596. Another of the Old Guard and a university trained writer. Peele is believed to be one of Shakespeare's early mentors, co-writing the early tragedy Titus Andronicus with the young William Shakespeare. Peele is believed to have written the first two acts and Shakespeare the remaining three.

Thomas Kyd - November 1585 – December 1600. Like Shakespeare Thomas Kyd did not come from a highly privileged background. He is most famous for his play The Spanish Tragedy 1587 approx, the first Elizabethan blockbuster and the first Elizabethan tragedy. His play would provide the template of all subsequent tragedy until Shakespeare radically changed the form with his Hamlet in 1599. He died after being arrested and probably tortured after blasphemous tracts were found in his lodgings, which he shared with Christopher Marlowe.

Christopher Marlowe - baptised 26 February 1564 – 30 May 1593. Another university trained writer. Marlowe was also a possible spy for Elizabeth I, he was an atheist, and a homosexual. He was arrested, probably after Kyd informed on him under torture, for blasphemous writings found in his lodgings. He was killed, by know government agents, in a brawl in Depford over a bar bill. Christopher Marlowe's plays are noted for their poetry as well as their extraordinary violence and cruelty.

William Shakespeare - 23 April 1564 – 23 April 1616. Actor, poet and playwright of 36 plays, 4 narrative poems and 154 Sonnets. Widely celebrated in his lifetime as a playwright with many of his plays finding their way into print during his lifetime. His collected works were published posthumously, in 1623 by his colleagues. 20 of the plays published in the first folio had never been published before. Shakespeare wrote the majority of his plays for the Chamberlain's/Kings Men, of whom he was a shareholder. He retired to his home town in 1613, a wealthy and respected man.

Benjamin Jonson - 11 June 1572 - 16 August 1637. Bricklayer, Soldier, actor, playwright, poet and writer of court masques. Ben Johnson was both a rival and friend to Shakespeare. A freelance writer, Johnson wrote for many theatre companies, including the Chamberlain's/King's Men, who performed his tragedy Sejanus as well as his comedies Every Man in His Humour, Volpone, or The Fox, The Alchemist. He was imprisoned twice for plays he wrote, the lost Isle Of Dogs with Thomas Nash, which drew the displeasure of Elizabeth I, and Eastwards Ho, which offended James I. This offence did not stop him becoming a major writer of court masques, a popular entertainment in the court of James I. He was also arrested for killing fellow writer Gabriel Spencer narrowly escaping the death penalty. He would write a dedicatory poem to Shakespeare published in the First folio in 1623.

Thomas Nashe – 1567 – 1601. Playwright, poet, satirist and pamphleteer. Nashe was a parson's son from Lowestoft, Suffolk. He received a Bachelor's degree from Cambridge university. Best remembered as the co-writer of the lost satirical play The Isle of Dogs with Ben Johnson. As well as a possible collaboration with Christopher Marlowe on Dido: Queen of Carthage. And as one of the playwrights including Shakespeare and Marlowe, who collaborated on Henry VI Part I.

Wanted

Name:
For:

Reward:

Stage: 4 **Topic: Shakespeare the reader** **Lesson: 11**

Learning Intention: What were Shakespeare's biggest influences? What was reading culture like in Elizabethan London.

Teaching strategy: Teacher directed learning and Student centred learning.

Presentation:

- Settle class and Roll.
- Teacher introduces the literary life of London. See teachers notes.
- Worksheet comparing Shakespeare's texts to the originals.
- Class discussion of why Shakespeare was able to do this? and Why he would do this at all?
- How is this different to how we think of writers now?
- Would Shakespeare be able to get away with this now? Why? Why not?
- Pack up

Lesson reflection:

Shakespeare and original texts.

Shakespeare lived at a time when books were beginning to become truly democratised. Increasing literacy meant that the traditional regulators of the public's reading – the Church, the Court and School – were losing their control over what people were able to read. English translations of ancient texts, such as Plutarch's Lives meant that readers, who could not read the original Latin text had access to these works for the first time. Shakespeare himself, read this text in English. Because of this democratisation of literacy, this period also saw increased censorship by both the Church and the Court, as a way of controlling the reading lives of the public. The Bishops Ban would put and end to English history plays in 1599. Other books and plays would be banned outright by the court.

Just as the appetite of the theatre going audiences, required the continual production of new plays, the appetite of the reading public saw a boom in publishing, both authorised and unauthorised. Shakespeare saw both his long narrative poems, Venus and Adonis and The Rape of Lucretia into print in 1593 and 1594. As well as being the victim of theft in 1599 with the publication of The Passionate Pilgrim, which included, deliberately bad poetry from his Love's Labours Lost, assorted other poems, by other writers and stolen sonnets. Shakespeare did not publish The sonnets in his lifetime, sharing them only with close friends.

From his works it is possible to recreate what Shakespeare read to produce his plays. Some of his most prominent sources appear to be Ovid's Metamorphoses, to which he returns repeatedly. Holinshed's Chronicles, the source for his English History plays. And Plutarch's Lives which provided direct inspiration for his two greatest Roman plays Julius Caesar and Antony and Cleopatra.

Compare and contrast Plutarch and Shakespeare.

Plutarch's Lives – Antony

She (Cleopatra) received several letters, both from Antony and from his friends, to summon her, but she took no account of these orders; and at last, as if in mockery of them, she came sailing up the river Cydnus, in a barge with gilded stern and outspread sails of purple, while oars of silver beat time to the music of flutes and fifes and harps. She herself lay all along, under a canopy of cloth of gold, dressed as Venus in a picture, and beautiful young boys, like painted Cupids, stood on each side to fan her. Her maids were dressed like Sea Nymphs and Graces, some steering at the rudder, some working at the ropes. The perfumes diffused themselves from the vessel to the shore, which was covered with multitudes, part following the galley up the river on either bank, part running out of the city to see the sight. The market-place was quite emptied, and Antony at last was left alone sitting upon the tribunal; while the word went through all the multitude, that Venus was come to feast with Bacchus, for the common good of Asia.

Antony and Cleopatra Act II Scene 2

ENOBARBUS.

I will tell you.

The barge she sat in, like a burnished throne,

Burned on the water. The poop was beaten gold;

Purple the sails, and so perfumed that

The winds were love-sick with them; the oars were silver,

Which to the tune of flutes kept stroke, and made

The water which they beat to follow faster,

As amorous of their strokes. For her own person,

It beggared all description: she did lie

In her pavilion, cloth-of-gold of tissue,

O'erpicturing that Venus where we see

The fancy outwork nature. On each side her

Stood pretty dimpled boys, like smiling Cupids,

With divers-coloured fans, whose wind did seem

To glow the delicate cheeks which they did cool,

And what they undid did.

AGRIPPA.

O, rare for Antony!

ENOBARBUS.

Her gentlewomen, like the Nereides,

So many mermaids, tended her i' th' eyes,

And made their bends adornings. At the helm

A seeming mermaid steers. The silken tackle

Swell with the touches of those flower-soft hands

That yarely frame the office. From the barge

A strange invisible perfume hits the sense

Of the adjacent wharfs. The city cast

Her people out upon her, and Antony,

Enthroned i' th' market-place, did sit alone,

Whistling to th' air, which, but for vacancy,

Had gone to gaze on Cleopatra too,

And made a gap in nature.

- How are the two texts similar?
- How do the two texts differ?
- How does Shakespeare change what Plutarch wrote?
- Why do you think he did this?

Stage: 4   **Topic:** I don't understand what they're saying! - Language
Lesson: 12

Learning Intention: Familiarising the students with Shakespeare's language. Is it really that hard, or does it just require skills to decipher and understand it.

Teaching strategy: Teacher directed class discussion and book work.
Presentation:
- Settle class and Roll.
- Introduce Topic: Are the actual words foreign to us or is it just a very knotty and dense way of speaking?
- Discuss the difference between specialised language and archaic language.
- Read Enobarb's speech from Antony and Cleopatra to the class.
- Students fill in the Archaic or Specialised language worksheet. For the weaker students this is best done as a class together. A stronger class should be given a chance to fill this in on their own and then discuss as a class after their solo attempts.
- Discuss the students findings.
- Ask the students if it is not the bulk of the words that are making this difficult to understand, what else is going on?
- Pack up
Lesson reflection:

I don't understand what they're saying – Language

ANTONY AND CLEOPATRA Act II Scene 2

ENOBARBUS.

When she first met Mark Antony, she pursed up his heart upon the river of Cydnus.

AGRIPPA.

There she appeared indeed, or my reporter devised well for her.

ENOBARBUS.

I will tell you.

The barge she sat in, like a burnished throne,

Burned on the water. The poop was beaten gold;

Purple the sails, and so perfumed that

The winds were love-sick with them; the oars were silver,

Which to the tune of flutes kept stroke, and made

The water which they beat to follow faster,

As amorous of their strokes. For her own person,

It beggared all description: she did lie

In her pavilion, cloth-of-gold of tissue,

O'erpicturing that Venus where we see

The fancy outwork nature. On each side her

Stood pretty dimpled boys, like smiling Cupids,

With divers-coloured fans, whose wind did seem

To glow the delicate cheeks which they did cool,

And what they undid did.

AGRIPPA.

O, rare for Antony!

ENOBARBUS.

Her gentlewomen, like the Nereides,

So many mermaids, tended her i' th' eyes,

And made their bends adornings. At the helm

A seeming mermaid steers. The silken tackle

Swell with the touches of those flower-soft hands

That yarely frame the office. From the barge

A strange invisible perfume hits the sense

Of the adjacent wharfs. The city cast

Her people out upon her, and Antony,

Enthroned i' th' market-place, did sit alone,

Whistling to th' air, which, but for vacancy,

Had gone to gaze on Cleopatra too,

And made a gap in nature.

AGRIPPA.

Rare Egyptian!

ENOBARBUS.

Upon her landing, Antony sent to her,

Invited her to supper. She replied

It should be better he became her guest,

Which she entreated. Our courteous Antony,

Whom ne'er the word of "No" woman heard speak,

Being barbered ten times o'er, goes to the feast,

And, for his ordinary, pays his heart

For what his eyes eat only.

AGRIPPA.

Royal wench!

She made great Caesar lay his sword to bed.

He ploughed her, and she cropped.

ENOBARBUS.

I saw her once

Hop forty paces through the public street

And, having lost her breath, she spoke and panted,

That she did make defect perfection,

And, breathless, pour breath forth.

MAECENAS.

Now Antony must leave her utterly.

ENOBARBUS.

Never. He will not.

Age cannot wither her, nor custom stale

Her infinite variety. Other women cloy

The appetites they feed, but she makes hungry

Where most she satisfies. For vilest things

Become themselves in her, that the holy priests

Bless her when she is riggish.

Archaic words	Specialised words	Meaning
Archaic words	Specialised words	Meaning

Stage: 4   Topic: I don't understand what they're saying! - Imagery
Lesson: 13

Learning Intention: Continuing on from last lesson, this lesson is looking at imagery and how that is used in Shakespeare's plays.

Teaching strategy: Teacher directed and independent work
Presentation:
- Settle class and Roll.
- What is imagery? Metaphor, Simile, Personification and Allusions.
- What do we know about the Elizabethan Stage that would make verbal imagery important?
- Imagery worksheet. Students identify imagery and compose their own using the forms discussed.

Extended Questions:
Identify the images in each quote.
How does the image help you understand the emotion or situation described?
What does it tell you about the Character?
Do these quotes rely on a single technique to create their image?
How does laying technique upon technique make the image more vivid?
Write your own description using the techniques discussed in class

Standard Questions:
Identify the images in each quote.
How does the image help you understand the emotion or situation described?
Write your own description using the techniques discussed in class

Supported Questions:
Identify the images in each quote.

How does the image make you feel?

Illustrate the central image from each quote.

What colours did you chose for each image, why?

Write your own description using the techniques discussed in class

- Have students share their own imagery.
- Pack up

Lesson reflection:

I don't understand what they're saying! - Imagery.

What is imagery? Imagery is a mental picture or a concrete representation of something.

Metaphor: Is a comparison that likens two things by identifying one with another. It comes from Greek meaning: to carry across.

I'll bury thee in a triumphant grave.
A grave? O no, a lantern, slaught'red youth,
For here lies Juliet, and her beauty makes
This vault a feasting presence full of light.   ROMEO AND JULIET

Here Romeo compares Juliet's beauty to a lantern, her presence makes the dark crypt a welcoming and friendly sight.

Simile: Is a comparison that likens two things by identifying one with another, but using a linking word to make the comparison clear. i.e. Like, as, such as, how.

O swear not by the moon, th'inconstant moon,
That monthly changes in her circled orb,
Lest that thy love prove likewise variable.   ROMEO AND JULIET

Juliet is telling Romeo not to swear that he loves her using something that changes like the moon, unless he means that his love will also change.

Personification: Giving non-human things, e.g. landscapes, animals, plants, buildings, emotions, human characteristics.

O, beware, my lord, of jealousy;
It is the green-ey'd monster which doth mock
The meat it feeds on.   OTHELLO

Jealousy is given the human characteristics of eating and mocking.

Allusions: References to other literary works, religious texts, myth, historical event or other cultural artifact to help reinforce meaning.

....and wither'd murder,
Alarum'd by his sentinel, the wolf,
Whose howl's his watch, thus with his stealthy pace,
With Tarquin's ravishing strides, towards his design
Moves like a ghost.   MACBETH

Tarquin was a character from Roman history, the third son of the last of the Ancient kings before the republic. He was welcomed into a friends house and assaulted his friend's wife, Lucretia. Shakespeare wants his audience to grasp how horrible what Macbeth is planning to do. King Duncan is a welcomed guest in Macbeth's house and now Macbeth is plotting to kill him in a place he should be safe. Just as Lucretia should have been safe.

Imagery

Over thy wounds now do I prophesy,
Which, like dumb mouths do ope their ruby lips
To beg the voice and utterance of my tongue,
                                          JULIUS CAESAR

Will all great Neptune's ocean wash this blood
Clean from my hand? No, this my hand will rather
The multitudinous seas incarnadine,
Making the green one red.
                                            MACBETH

When down her weedy trophies and herself
Fell in the weeping brook. Her clothes spread wide,
And mermaid-like, awhile they bore her up,
Which time she chanted snatches of old tunes,
As one incapable of her own distress,
Or like a creature native and indued
Unto that element. But long it could not be
Till that her garments, heavy with their drink,
Pull'd the poor wretch from her melodious lay
To muddy death.
                                            HAMLET

So, when he had occasion to be seen,
He was but as the cuckoo is in June,
Heard, not regarded; seen, but with such eyes
As, sick and blunted with community,
Afford no extraordinary gaze,
Such as is bent on sun-like majesty
When it shines seldom in admiring eyes;
But rather drowsed, and hung their eyelids down,
Slept in his face, and render'd such aspect
As cloudy men use to their adversaries,
Being with his presence glutted, gorged, and full.
                                            HENRY IV PART 1

for if you hide the crown
Even in your hearts, there will he rake for it.
Therefore in fierce tempest is he coming,
In thunder and in earthquake, like a Jove,
                                            HENRY V

Now is the winter of our discontent
Made glorious summer by this sun of York;
And all the clouds that lour'd upon our house
In the deep bosom of the ocean buried.
                                            RICHARD III

When we have laugh'd to see the sails conceive,
And grow big-bellied with the wanton wind;
Which she, with pretty and with swimming gait
Following (her womb then rich with my young squire),
Would imitate, and sail upon the land,
To fetch me trifles, and return again,
As from a voyage, rich with merchandise.

                                            A MIDSUMMERS NIGHT'S DREAM

Stage: 4   Topic: I don't understand what they're saying! - Wordplay and Puns   Lesson: 14

Learning Intention: Continuing on from the last lesson looking at how Wordplay and Puns create humour.

Teaching strategy: Teacher directed and independent work
Presentation:
- Settle class and Roll.
- Introduce the concept of Wordplay and Punning. Class notes
- Wordplay worksheet.
- Discuss the student's answers and why they think so much of the comedy is verbal.
-Pack up
Lesson reflection:

Wordplay and Puns

Comedy in Shakespeare's plays is more often created through the verbal interchanges of the characters than through action. Physical comedy was a part of the stage craft of the Elizabethan theatre, with professional clowns being a highlight for many theatre goers. However their performances were improvised as were some of their lines. As a playwright Shakespeare creates comedy through his words.
We will be looking at three types of wordplay that Shakespeare employed.

Malapropisms: A malapropism is the mistaken use of a word in place of a word that sounds similar for comic effect. In Shakespeare this generally occurs when a low status character is speaking to a higher status character and is trying to sound more learned than he or she is.

Puns: Puns are a humorous play on words that exploit the multiple meanings of the word. Some of the easiest to identify are homophones. Words that sound the same, but have different meanings. E.g. waste and waist. Homographs are words that are spelt the same with different meanings. E.g. read and read. (You had to read that twice to get your emphasis right didn't you?)

Bombast: Pompous or extravagant language. This can also result in malapropisms. E.g. Captain Fluellen in Henry V doesn't say that the enemy losses at the bridge are great he says: *The perdition* (damnation) *of the adversary hath been very great, reasonable great.*

Comedy is often played out in scenes where there is one straight character trying to get a straight answer out of a comic character. Look at the brief passage between The Chief Justice a straight character and Sir John Falstaff, a comic character. Note how Falstaff turns the Chief Justice's lines into puns, and bombast's his way out of actually answering any questions.

CHIEF JUSTICE.
Well, the truth is, Sir John, you live in great infamy.

FALSTAFF.
He that buckles himself in my belt cannot live in less.

CHIEF JUSTICE.
Your means are very slender, and your waste is great.

FALSTAFF.
I would it were otherwise; I would my means were greater and my waist slenderer.

CHIEF JUSTICE.
You have misled the youthful Prince.

FALSTAFF.
The young Prince hath misled me. I am the fellow with the great belly, and he my dog.

CHIEF JUSTICE.
Well, I am loath to gall a new-heal'd wound. Your day's service at Shrewsbury hath a little gilded over your night's exploit on Gadshill. You may thank th' unquiet time for your quiet o'erposting that action.

FALSTAFF.
My lord-

CHIEF JUSTICE.
But since all is well, keep it so: wake not a sleeping wolf.

FALSTAFF.
To wake a wolf is as bad as smell a fox.   HENRY IV PART 2

Identify the techniques used in the following quotes. Then write your own dialogue of no more than 5 lines using at least two of the techniques looked at today.

GOWER.
Captain Fluellen!

FLUELLEN.
So! in the name of Jesu Christ, speak lower. It is the greatest admiration in the

universal world, when the true and ancient prerogatives and laws of the wars is not kept. If you would take the pains but to examine the wars of Pompey the Great, you shall find, I warrant you, that there is no tiddle taddle nor pibble pabble in Pompey's camp. I warrant you, you shall find the ceremonies of the wars, and the cares of it, and the forms of it, and the sobriety of it, and the modesty of it, to be otherwise.

GOWER.
Why, the enemy is loud; you hear him all night.

FLUELLEN.
If the enemy is an ass and a fool and a prating coxcomb, is it meet, think you, that we should also, look you, be an ass and a fool and a prating coxcomb? In your own conscience, now?

GOWER.
I will speak lower. HENRY V

LEONATO.
Go, I discharge thee of thy prisoner, and I thank thee.

DOGBERRY.
I leave an arrant knave with your worship; which I beseech your worship to correct yourself, for the example of others. God keep your worship! I wish your worship well; God restore you to health! I humbly give you leave to depart, and if a merry meeting may be wished, God prohibit it! Come, neighbour.
MUCH ADO ABOUT NOTHING

MERCUTIO.
Come, come, thou art as hot a Jack in thy mood as any in Italy; and as soon moved to be moody, and as soon moody to be moved. ROMEO AND JULIET

VIOLA.
Save thee, friend, and thy music. Dost thou live by thy tabor?

CLOWN.
No, sir, I live by the church.

VIOLA.
Art thou a churchman?

CLOWN.
No such matter, sir. I do live by the church, for I do live at my house, and my house doth stand by the church. TWELFTH NIGHT OR
WHAT YOU WILL.

Stage: 4　Topic: I don't understand what they're saying! - Verse and prose　Lesson: 15

Learning Intention: Continuing on from the last lesson, identifying Verse and Prose and why both are used and in what contexts.

Teaching strategy: Teacher directed discussion and Student centred work.

Presentation:

- Settle class and Roll.
- Notes What is verse/prose? Some plays are entirely in verse, others prose, others are a mix.
- Have class speak some examples of each. What did they notice?
- Verse/Prose worksheet.
- Pack up

Lesson reflection:

I Don't understand what they're saying - Verse and Prose

Verse refers to poetical writing with a metrical rhythm, often ending in a rhyme. Blank verse refers to poetical writing with a metrical rhythm that does not end in a rhyme. Prose is written or spoken language that follows the natural flow of speech. During the Elizabethan period, the language of plays had gradually changed from the strict use of only verse to a combination of verse and prose. This can be seen not only in the work of Shakespeare, but also his contemporaries like Marlowe, Johnson, Kyd and others. Some of Shakespeare's plays are written entirely or almost entirely in verse, e.g. Richard II and Titus Andronicus. Others are almost entirely in prose, eg As You Like It or The Merry Wives of Windsor. Most however are a combination of the two.

In general verse is used to differentiate the speech of high status characters from low status characters, who speak prose. However, this is not the only way that verse and prose can be used in these plays. In The Taming of the Shrew, Petruchio and Katherine speak verse to one another, until they develop an intimacy that allows them to speak to each other in prose. Hamlet, speaks verse when in formal occasions, but when pretending to be mad or when overcome by emotion slips into prose.

Blank verse, also called iambic pentameter, is a rhythmic type of verse that was developed in written English by Chaucer in the Middle ages. Thomas Kyd was the first to use it on the stage in his play The Spanish Tragedy. Shakespeare uses Blank verse, and Iambic pentameter sometimes seriously, as in Romeo and Juliet, where the lovers language is strictly rhythmical, but he will also put it into the mouths of fools like in the mechanical's play in A Midsummers Night's Dream where he is mocking the artificiality of it. Or into the mouths of Macbeth's witches where it makes them sound creepy and otherworldly.

Examples of Verse:

But soft, what light through yonder window breaks?
It is the east, and Juliet is the sun!
                                        ROMEO AND JULIET

Let's talk of graves, of worms, and epitaphs,
Make dust our paper, and with rainy eyes
Write sorrow on the bosom of the earth.
                                        RICHARD II

The King doth keep his revels here tonight;
Take heed the Queen come not within his sight,
For Oberon is passing fell and wrath,
Because that she, as her attendant, hath
                                        A MIDSUMMERS NIGHT'S DREAM

Examples of Prose:

QUINCE.
You, Nick Bottom, are set down for Pyramus.
BOTTOM.
What is Pyramus—a lover, or a tyrant?
QUINCE.
A lover, that kills himself most gallantly for love.
BOTTOM.
That will ask some tears in the true performing of it. If I do it, let the audience look to their eyes. I will move storms; I will condole in some measure. To the rest—yet my chief humour is for a tyrant. I could play Ercles rarely, or a part to tear a cat in, to make all split.

A MIDSUMMERS NIGHT'S DREAM

BENEDICK.
I do love nothing in the world so well as you: is not that strange?
BEATRICE.
As strange as the thing I know not. It were as possible for me to say I loved nothing so well as you; but believe me not, and yet I lie not; I confess nothing, nor I deny nothing. I am sorry for my cousin.
BENEDICK.
By my sword, Beatrice, thou lovest me.

MUCH ADO ABOUT NOTHING

KING HENRY.
I myself heard the King say he would not be ransom'd.
WILLIAMS.
Ay, he said so, to make us fight cheerfully; but when our throats are cut, he may be ransom'd, and we ne'er the wiser.
KING HENRY.
If I live to see it, I will never trust his word after.

HENRY V

What do you notice about the difference between the two types of writing?

Choose one of the examples of verse what is the emotion the piece evokes? Now play with the stress and tempo to create a different emotion and a different emphasis from the original.

This is part of the scene of the Witches in their cave brewing up a potion.

SECOND WITCH.
Fillet of a fenny snake,
In the cauldron boil and bake;
Eye of newt, and toe of frog,
Wool of bat, and tongue of dog,
Adder's fork, and blind-worm's sting,
Lizard's leg, and howlet's wing,
For a charm of powerful trouble,
Like a hell-broth boil and bubble.
ALL.
Double, double, toil and trouble;
Fire, burn; and cauldron, bubble.
                                        MACBETH

The Duke of Illyria is in love with a lady who does not return his affection.

DUKE.
If music be the food of love, play on,
Give me excess of it; that, surfeiting,
The appetite may sicken and so die.
That strain again, it had a dying fall;
O, it came o'er my ear like the sweet sound
That breathes upon a bank of violets,
Stealing and giving odour. Enough; no more;
'Tis not so sweet now as it was before.
O spirit of love, how quick and fresh art thou,
That notwithstanding thy capacity
Receiveth as the sea, nought enters there,
Of what validity and pitch soever,
But falls into abatement and low price
Even in a minute! So full of shapes is fancy,
That it alone is high fantastical.
                        TWELFTH NIGHT OR WHAT YOU WILL.

Hamlet has just seen his recently deceased father's ghost.

HAMLET.
Angels and ministers of grace defend us!
Be thou a spirit of health or goblin damn'd,
Bring with thee airs from heaven or blasts from hell,
Be thy intents wicked or charitable,
Thou com'st in such a questionable shape

That I will speak to thee. I'll call thee Hamlet,
King, father, royal Dane. O, answer me!
Let me not burst in ignorance; but tell
Why thy canoniz'd bones, hearsed in death,
Have burst their cerements; why the sepulchre,
Wherein we saw thee quietly inurn'd,
Hath op'd his ponderous and marble jaws
To cast thee up again! What may this mean,
That thou, dead corse, again in complete steel,
Revisit'st thus the glimpses of the moon,
Making night hideous, and we fools of nature
So horridly to shake our disposition
With thoughts beyond the reaches of our souls?
Say, why is this? Wherefore? What should we do?
HAMLET

Helena believes that her friend Hermia has used her power over the two men who love her, to tease Helena.

HELENA.
O spite! O hell! I see you all are bent
To set against me for your merriment.
If you were civil, and knew courtesy,
You would not do me thus much injury.
Can you not hate me, as I know you do,
But you must join in souls to mock me too?
If you were men, as men you are in show,
You would not use a gentle lady so;
To vow, and swear, and superpraise my parts,
When I am sure you hate me with your hearts.
You both are rivals, and love Hermia;
And now both rivals, to mock Helena.
A trim exploit, a manly enterprise,
To conjure tears up in a poor maid's eyes
With your derision! None of noble sort
Would so offend a virgin, and extort
A poor soul's patience, all to make you sport.
A MIDSUMMERS NIGHT'S DREAM

Stage: 4   Topic: I don't understand what they're saying! - Insults
Lesson: 16

Learning Intention: Continuing on from the last lesson looking at how Shakespeare manages to create language that is both insulting and not swearing.

Teaching strategy: Teacher directed discussion and Student centred work.

Presentation:
- Settle class and Roll.
- Intro to insults. Teacher talk
- Insults worksheet
- Students compose their own insults in Shakespeare's style and share. Don't share the insults if you have a class that is socially dysfunctional, this is meant to be fun, not bullying.
- Class discussion on why these are effective and funny, without swearing.
- Pack up

Lesson reflection:

Teacher's notes

Shakespeare's plays are full of insults. These insults often bring together all the language forms that we have studied so far. They are generally complex images, that an actor can use to both express their character's displeasure or anger and can provoke a reaction in both their scene partner and the audience. The basic formula for a Shakespearean insult is: Adjective (Describing word) + compound Adjective + Noun (naming word) = insult.

Insults also take the form word play and puns.

Elizabethan theatre audiences clearly enjoyed this kind of verbal humour. And this form of humour was tolerated by the official censor. Other forms of humour, such as profanity, which in Shakespeare's day meant religious oaths, such as Swounds, which means God's Wounds, came under increasing scrutiny. As Religious fundamentalism and political tensions around a proposed union of England and Scotland grew across the country, parliamentarians focused increasingly on the theatre leading to an outright ban on swearing in all theatres in May of 1606. The result of the 'Act to Restrain the Abuses of Players' could see an actor fined ten pounds, or half a years wages. Punning insults that did not mention God, were unaffected and continued to be included in the later plays of Shakespeare.

Thus an insult like "Thou art a boil, a plague sore" from King Lear, would cause no offence, but an innocent seeming line like "But keep your way, i' God's name; I have done." from, Much ado about Nothing, would have to read: "But keep your way, I have done."

Shakespeare's choicest insults

Never hung poison on a fouler toad.
Out of my sight! Thou dost infect mine eyes.   RICHARD III

CHIRON. Thou hast undone our mother.
AARON. Villain, I have done thy mother.   TITUS ANDRONICUS

More of your conversation
would infect my brain, being the herdsmen of the beastly
plebeians. I will be bold to take my leave of you.   CORIOLANUS

The plague of Greece upon thee, thou mongrel beef-witted lord!   TROILUS AND CRESSIDA

I would thou didst itch from head to foot and I had the scratching of thee; I would make thee the loathsomest scab in Greece.   TROILUS AND CRESSIDA

if he were opened and you find so much blood in his liver as will clog the foot of a flea,   TWELFTH NIGHT

But it is certain that when he makes
water his urine is congeal'd ice; that I know to be true.   MEASURE FOR MEASURE

Thou elvish-mark'd, abortive, rooting hog!   RICHARD III

Thou leathern-jerkin, crystal-button, knot-pated, agatering, puke-stocking, caddis-garter, smooth-tongue, Spanish pouch!   HENRY IV PART 1

Thou art a boil, a plague sore   KING LEAR

PRINCE.
I'll be no longer guilty of this sin; this sanguine coward, this bed-presser, this horse-back-breaker, this huge hill of flesh,—

FALSTAFF.
Away, you starveling, you eel-skin, you dried neat's-tongue, you
stock-fish,—
O, for breath to utter what is like thee!—you tailor's-yard, you
sheath, you bow-case, you vile standing tuck,—

PRINCE.
Well, breathe awhile, and then to it again: and, when thou hast tired thyself in base comparisons,   HENRY IV PART 1

Take one word from each column to create a unique Shakespearean style insult. Remember to think of the image you are creating when you chose your words e.g Unmuzzled, rude-growling, flap-dragon.

Adjective	Compound Adjective	Noun
Artless	Bat-fowling	Apple-john
Bawdy	Beetle-headed	Baggage
Beslubbering	Boil-brained	Barnacle
Bootless	Clapper-clawed	Bladder
Churlish	Clay-brained	Boar-pig
Cockered	Common-kissing	Bugbear
Craven	Dismal-dreaming	Canker-blossom
Decayed	Dizzy-eyed	Clotpole
Dissembling	Dog-hearted	Codpiece
Droning	Earth-vexing	Coxcomb
Errant	Eel-skinned	Death-token
Execrable	Fat-kidneyed	Dewberry
Fawning	Fen-sucked	Fancy-monger
Fishified	Flap-mouthed	Flap-dragon
Fobbing	Fly-bitten	Flax-wench
Forward	Fool-born	Flibbertigibbert
Giddy	Foul-spoken	Flirt-gill
Gleeking	Full-gorged	Foot-licker
Goatish	Guts-gripping	Fragment
Impertinant	Hare-brained	Gudgeon
Infectious	Hasty-witted	Haggard
Juggling	Hedge-born	Harpy
Languageless	Hell-hated	Hedge-pig
Loggerheaded	Idle-headed	Horn-beast
Lumpish	Ill-breeding	Horse-drench
Malicious	Knotty-pated	Hugger-mugger
Mangled	Lilly-livered	Lewdstar
Mewling	Long-tonged	Lout
Paunchy	Malmsy-nosed	Maggot-pie
Punny	Marble-hearted	Malt-worm
Odiferous	Nimble-footed	Measle
Qualling	Onion-eyed	Minnow
Rank	Plume-plucked	Miscreant
Reeky	Pox-marked	Mouldwarp
Roguish	Puppy-headed	Mumble-news
Saucy	Reeling-ripe	Pigeon-egg
Scurvy	Rough-hewn	Pignut
Spleeny	Rude-growling	Popinjay
Spongy	Skimble-skamble	Promise-breaker
Surly	Sheep-biting	Pumpkin
Unmuzzled	Super-serviceable	Ratsbane
Venomed	Tardy-gaited	Shrimp
Villainous	Tickle-brained	Strumpet
Viperous	Toad-spotted	Time-pleaser
Wayward	Unwash'd	Toad
Weedy	Wasp-stung	Whey-face
Yeasty	Weather-bitten	Wagtail

Stage: 4   Topic: Categories Comedy, History and Tragedy
Lesson: 17

Learning Intention: Understanding the different categories of the plays: Comedy History and Tragedy.

Teaching strategy: Teacher directed notes and discussion
Presentation:
- Settle class and Roll.
- Brainstorm with the class the concept of genres and how they help and audience understand what they are watching. Try and list as many different types of genre and the audience expectation from that genre. e.g. Romance will generally have a misunderstanding and will end with the couple getting together
- What are the categories of the plays? Class notes
- Pack up
Lesson reflection:

Comedy, History, Tragedy.

Today, we group Shakespeare's plays into three categories, Comedy, History and Tragedy. These were the categories that the plays were grouped into by the compilers of the First Folio in 1623. However Shakespeare himself would not have understood his plays to sit within such rigid boundaries. For instance a play that we call a history play Richard III is fully described as a tragedy. Another History play Henry IV parts 1 and 2 are both history plays and comedies. In Hamlet Shakespeare himself gives us a comic rendition of the wide variety of play genres fashionable in the theatre while he was working, when Polonius introduces the actors to the court.

"The best actors in the world, either for tragedy, comedy, history, pastoral, pastoral-comical, historical-pastoral, tragical-historical, tragical-comical-historical-pastoral, scene individable, or poem unlimited." HAMLET ACT II SCENE 2.

As we have been left only the designations, Comedy, History and Tragedy, these are the ones we must work with.

The Comedies are the plays that generally focus on courtship and usually end with marriage. Their drama is predicated upon misunderstanding and confusion, that can be easily untangled. The stakes can be quite high, but the resolution is always peaceful and non-violent. The focus of the comedies is the restoration of order that has some how been disrupted at the outset or during the beginning of the play. For instance, two sets of identical twins, separated at birth being mistaken for the other as in The Comedy of Errors. Some of the Comedies can be quite dark, but they are always resolved without bloodshed.

The History plays refer to the plays directly inspired by the history of the Kings of England. These are mostly grouped into two long cycles of plays: The Henriad refering to the four plays: Richard II, Henry IV Parts 1 and 2 and Henry V. And the cycle of plays that makes up Henry VI Parts 1, 2, and 3 and Richard III, which can be called The Margaretsaga. As well as Henry VIII and King John. These plays all relate to actual kings of England, and look at ideas of What makes a 'good' king? By what right does a monarch rule? and Under what circumstances are they allowed to be deposed?

The Tragedies all follow the idea that a fatal flaw or grievous error causes the downfall and suffering of the tragic hero. The exception to this model is the revenge tragedy, which was popular from the 1580's, this type of tragedy involves a wrong being committed against the tragic hero, who must avenge the wrong even at the cost of their own lives. Titus Andronicus, with its tit for tat cruelty and killings is an example of this style of tragedy. Hamlet, wrestling with his ghostly father's injunction to avenge him is also considered a revenge tragedy. Other tragedies, like Romeo and Juliet, or Othello are created through misunderstanding or manipulation. The moment blood is shed in a tragedy it can only end one way. Because of the propensity of Elizabethan audiences to wander away once their favourite actor had left the stage, the deaths in Shakespearean tragedies are always placed at the very end of the play.

Stage: 4   Topic: Categories Comedy, History and Tragedy
Lesson: 18

Learning Intention: Understanding the different categories of the plays: Comedy.

Teaching strategy: Teacher directed notes and discussion with questions.

Presentation:
- Settle class and Roll.
- Hand out your chosen play script (You only need to use one of the three options provided.) and Read or watch play extract
- After watching give the students the following questions:
These questions can be answered as a class on the board or in pairs in their books and then bring the class back together to discuss their answers.
- What is happening?
- What techniques are being used?
- What makes it Comedy/ History/Tragedy?
- Do elements from other genres enter?
- How might the staging emphasise the genre?
- Pack up

Lesson reflection:

Comedies

Much Ado About Nothing.

ACT IV SCENE II. A Prison.

Enter Dogberry, Verges, and Sexton, in gowns; and the Watch, with Conrade and Borachio.

DOGBERRY.

Is our whole dissembly appeared?

VERGES.

O! a stool and a cushion for the sexton.

SEXTON.

Which be the malefactors?

DOGBERRY.

Marry, that am I and my partner.

VERGES.

Nay, that's certain: we have the exhibition to examine.

SEXTON.

But which are the offenders that are to be examined? let them come before Master Constable.

DOGBERRY.

Yea, marry, let them come before me. What is your name, friend?

BORACHIO.

Borachio.

DOGBERRY.

Pray write down Borachio. Yours, sirrah?

CONRADE.

I am a gentleman, sir, and my name is Conrade.

DOGBERRY.

Write down Master gentleman Conrade. Masters, do you serve God?

BOTH.

Yea, sir, we hope.

DOGBERRY.

Write down that they hope they serve God: and write God first; for God defend but God should go before such villains! Masters, it is proved already that you are little better than false knaves, and it will go near to be thought so shortly. How answer you for yourselves?

CONRADE.

Marry, sir, we say we are none.

DOGBERRY.

A marvellous witty fellow, I assure you; but I will go about with him. Come you hither, sirrah; a word in your ear: sir, I say to you, it is thought you are false knaves.

BORACHIO.

Sir, I say to you we are none.

DOGBERRY.

Well, stand aside. Fore God, they are both in a tale. Have you writ down, that they are none?

SEXTON.

Master Constable, you go not the way to examine: you must call forth the watch that are their accusers.

DOGBERRY.

Yea, marry, that's the eftest way. Let the watch come forth. Masters, I charge you, in the Prince's name, accuse these men.

FIRST WATCH.

This man said, sir, that Don John, the Prince's brother, was a villain.

DOGBERRY.

Write down Prince John a villain. Why, this is flat perjury, to call a Prince's brother villain.

BORACHIO.

Master Constable,—

DOGBERRY.

Pray thee, fellow, peace: I do not like thy look, I promise thee.

SEXTON.

What heard you him say else?

SECOND WATCH.

Marry, that he had received a thousand ducats of Don John for accusing the Lady Hero wrongfully.

DOGBERRY.

Flat burglary as ever was committed.

VERGES.

Yea, by the mass, that it is.

SEXTON.

What else, fellow?

FIRST WATCH.

And that Count Claudio did mean, upon his words, to disgrace Hero before the whole assembly, and not marry her.

DOGBERRY.

O villain! thou wilt be condemned into everlasting redemption for this.

SEXTON.

What else?

SECOND WATCH.

This is all.

SEXTON.

And this is more, masters, than you can deny. Prince John is this morning secretly stolen away: Hero was in this manner accused, in this manner refused, and, upon the grief of this, suddenly died. Master Constable, let these men be bound, and brought to Leonato's: I will go before and show him their examination.

[Exit.]

DOGBERRY.

Come, let them be opinioned.

VERGES.

Let them be in the hands—

CONRADE.

Off, coxcomb!

DOGBERRY.

God's my life! where's the sexton? let him write down the Prince's officer coxcomb. Come, bind them. Thou naughty varlet!

CONRADE.

Away! you are an ass; you are an ass.

DOGBERRY.

Dost thou not suspect my place? Dost thou not suspect my years? O that he were here to write me down an ass! but, masters, remember that I am an ass; though it be not written down, yet forget not that I am an ass. No, thou villain, thou art full of piety, as shall be proved upon thee by good witness. I am a wise fellow; and, which is more, an officer; and, which is more, a householder; and, which is more, as pretty a piece of flesh as any in Messina; and one that knows the law, go to; and a rich fellow enough, go to; and a fellow that hath had losses; and one that hath two gowns, and everything handsome about him. Bring him away. O that I had been writ down an ass!

Twelfth Night

ACT II SCENE V. Olivia's garden.

Enter Sir Toby, Sir Andrew and Fabian.

SIR TOBY.

Come thy ways, Signior Fabian.

FABIAN.

Nay, I'll come. If I lose a scruple of this sport, let me be boiled to death with melancholy.

SIR TOBY.

Wouldst thou not be glad to have the niggardly rascally sheep-biter come by some notable shame?

FABIAN.

I would exult, man. You know he brought me out o' favour with my lady about a bear-baiting here.

SIR TOBY.

To anger him we'll have the bear again, and we will fool him black and blue, shall we not, Sir Andrew?

SIR ANDREW.

And we do not, it is pity of our lives.

Enter Maria.

SIR TOBY.

Here comes the little villain. How now, my metal of India?

MARIA.

Get ye all three into the box-tree. Malvolio's coming down this walk; he has been yonder i' the sun practising behaviour to his own shadow this half hour: observe him, for the love of mockery; for I know this letter will make a contemplative idiot of him. Close, in the name of jesting! [The men hide themselves.] Lie thou there; [Throws down a letter] for here comes the trout that must be caught with tickling.

[Exit Maria.]

Enter Malvolio.

MALVOLIO.

'Tis but fortune, all is fortune. Maria once told me she did affect me, and I have heard herself come thus near, that should she fancy, it should be one of my complexion. Besides, she uses me with a more exalted respect than anyone else that follows her. What should I think on't?

SIR TOBY.

Here's an overweening rogue!

FABIAN.

O, peace! Contemplation makes a rare turkey-cock of him; how he jets under his advanced plumes!

SIR ANDREW.

'Slight, I could so beat the rogue!

SIR TOBY.

Peace, I say.

MALVOLIO.

To be Count Malvolio.

SIR TOBY.

Ah, rogue!

SIR ANDREW.

Pistol him, pistol him.

SIR TOBY.

Peace, peace.

MALVOLIO.

There is example for't. The lady of the Strachy married the yeoman of the wardrobe.

SIR ANDREW.

Fie on him, Jezebel!

FABIAN.

O, peace! now he's deeply in; look how imagination blows him.

MALVOLIO.

Having been three months married to her, sitting in my state—

SIR TOBY.

O for a stone-bow to hit him in the eye!

MALVOLIO.

Calling my officers about me, in my branched velvet gown; having come from a day-bed, where I have left Olivia sleeping.

SIR TOBY.

Fire and brimstone!

FABIAN.

O, peace, peace.

MALVOLIO.

And then to have the humour of state; and after a demure travel of regard, telling them I know my place as I would they should do theirs, to ask for my kinsman Toby.

SIR TOBY.

Bolts and shackles!

FABIAN.

O, peace, peace, peace! Now, now.

MALVOLIO.

Seven of my people, with an obedient start, make out for him. I frown the while, and perchance wind up my watch, or play with some rich jewel. Toby approaches; curtsies there to me—

SIR TOBY.

Shall this fellow live?

FABIAN.

Though our silence be drawn from us with cars, yet peace!

MALVOLIO.

I extend my hand to him thus, quenching my familiar smile with an austere regard of control—

SIR TOBY.

And does not Toby take you a blow o' the lips then?

MALVOLIO.

Saying 'Cousin Toby, my fortunes having cast me on your niece, give me this prerogative of speech—'

SIR TOBY.

What, what?

MALVOLIO.

'You must amend your drunkenness.'

SIR TOBY.

Out, scab!

FABIAN.

Nay, patience, or we break the sinews of our plot.

MALVOLIO.

'Besides, you waste the treasure of your time with a foolish knight—'

SIR ANDREW.

That's me, I warrant you.

MALVOLIO.

'One Sir Andrew.'

SIR ANDREW.

I knew 'twas I, for many do call me fool.

MALVOLIO.

[Taking up the letter.] What employment have we here?

FABIAN.

Now is the woodcock near the gin.

SIR TOBY.

O, peace! And the spirit of humours intimate reading aloud to him!

MALVOLIO.

By my life, this is my lady's hand: these be her very C's, her U's, and her T's, and thus makes she her great P's. It is in contempt of question, her hand.

SIR ANDREW.

Her C's, her U's, and her T's. Why that?

MALVOLIO.

[Reads.] To the unknown beloved, this, and my good wishes. Her very phrases! By your leave, wax. Soft! and the impressure her Lucrece, with which she uses to seal: 'tis my lady. To whom should this be?

FABIAN.

This wins him, liver and all.

MALVOLIO.

[Reads.]

    Jove knows I love,

    But who?

    Lips, do not move,

    No man must know.

'No man must know.' What follows? The numbers alter'd! 'No man must know.'—If this should be thee, Malvolio?

SIR TOBY.

Marry, hang thee, brock!

MALVOLIO.

> I may command where I adore,
>
> But silence, like a Lucrece knife,
>
> With bloodless stroke my heart doth gore;
>
> M.O.A.I. doth sway my life.

FABIAN.

A fustian riddle!

SIR TOBY.

Excellent wench, say I.

MALVOLIO.

'M.O.A.I. doth sway my life.'—Nay, but first let me see, let me see, let me see.

FABIAN.

What dish o' poison has she dressed him!

SIR TOBY.

And with what wing the staniel checks at it!

MALVOLIO.

'I may command where I adore.' Why, she may command me: I serve her, she is my lady. Why, this is evident to any formal capacity. There is no obstruction in this. And the end—what should that alphabetical position portend? If I could make that resemble something in me! Softly! 'M.O.A.I.'—

SIR TOBY.

O, ay, make up that:—he is now at a cold scent.

FABIAN.

Sowter will cry upon't for all this, though it be as rank as a fox.

MALVOLIO.

'M'—Malvolio; 'M!' Why, that begins my name!

FABIAN.

Did not I say he would work it out? The cur is excellent at faults.

MALVOLIO.

'M'—But then there is no consonancy in the sequel; that suffers under probation: 'A' should follow, but 'O' does.

FABIAN.

And 'O' shall end, I hope.

SIR TOBY.

Ay, or I'll cudgel him, and make him cry 'O!'

MALVOLIO.

And then 'I' comes behind.

FABIAN.

Ay, and you had any eye behind you, you might see more detraction at your heels than fortunes before you.

MALVOLIO.

'M.O.A.I.' This simulation is not as the former: and yet, to crush this a little, it would bow to me, for every one of these letters are in my name. Soft, here follows prose.

[Reads.] If this fall into thy hand, revolve. In my stars I am above thee, but be not afraid of greatness. Some are born great, some achieve greatness, and some have greatness thrust upon 'em. Thy fates open their hands, let thy blood and spirit embrace them. And, to inure thyself to what thou art like to be, cast thy humble slough and appear fresh. Be opposite with a kinsman, surly with servants. Let thy tongue tang arguments of state; put thyself into the trick of singularity. She thus advises thee that sighs for thee. Remember who commended thy yellow stockings, and wished to see thee ever cross-gartered. I say, remember. Go to, thou art made, if thou desir'st to be so. If not, let me see thee a steward still, the fellow of servants, and not worthy to touch Fortune's fingers. Farewell. She that would alter services with thee,

                The Fortunate Unhappy.

Daylight and champian discovers not more! This is open. I will be proud, I will read politic authors, I will baffle Sir Toby, I will wash off gross acquaintance, I will be point-device, the very man. I do not now fool myself, to let imagination jade me; for every reason excites to this, that my lady loves me. She did commend my yellow stockings of late, she did praise my leg being cross-gartered, and in this she manifests herself to my love, and with a kind of injunction, drives me to these habits of her liking. I thank my stars, I am happy. I will be strange, stout, in yellow stockings, and cross-gartered, even with the swiftness of putting on. Jove and my stars be praised!—Here is yet a postscript. [Reads.] Thou canst not choose but know who I am. If thou entertain'st my love, let it appear in thy smiling; thy smiles become thee well. Therefore in my presence still smile, dear my sweet, I prithee. Jove, I thank thee. I will smile, I will do everything that thou wilt have me.

[Exit.]

FABIAN.

I will not give my part of this sport for a pension of thousands to be paid from the Sophy.

SIR TOBY.

I could marry this wench for this device.

SIR ANDREW.

So could I too.

SIR TOBY.

And ask no other dowry with her but such another jest.

Enter Maria.

SIR ANDREW.

Nor I neither.

FABIAN.

Here comes my noble gull-catcher.

SIR TOBY.

Wilt thou set thy foot o' my neck?

SIR ANDREW.

Or o' mine either?

SIR TOBY.

Shall I play my freedom at tray-trip, and become thy bond-slave?

SIR ANDREW.

I' faith, or I either?

SIR TOBY.

Why, thou hast put him in such a dream, that when the image of it leaves him he must run mad.

MARIA.

Nay, but say true, does it work upon him?

SIR TOBY.

Like aqua-vitae with a midwife.

MARIA.

If you will then see the fruits of the sport, mark his first approach before my lady: he will come to her in yellow stockings, and 'tis a colour she abhors, and cross-gartered, a fashion she detests; and he will smile upon her, which will now be so unsuitable to her disposition, being addicted to a melancholy as she is, that it cannot but turn him into a notable contempt. If you will see it, follow me.

SIR TOBY.

To the gates of Tartar, thou most excellent devil of wit!

SIR ANDREW.

I'll make one too.

A Midsummers Night's Dream

ACT III SCENE I. The Wood.

The Queen of Fairies still lying asleep.

Enter Bottom, Quince, Snout, Starveling, Snug and Flute.

BOTTOM.

Are we all met?

QUINCE.

Pat, pat; and here's a marvellous convenient place for our rehearsal. This green plot shall be our stage, this hawthorn brake our tiring-house; and we will do it in action, as we will do it before the Duke.

BOTTOM.

Peter Quince?

QUINCE.

What sayest thou, bully Bottom?

BOTTOM.

There are things in this comedy of Pyramus and Thisbe that will never please. First, Pyramus must draw a sword to kill himself; which the ladies cannot abide. How answer you that?

SNOUT

By'r lakin, a parlous fear.

STARVELING.

I believe we must leave the killing out, when all is done.

BOTTOM.

Not a whit; I have a device to make all well. Write me a prologue, and let the prologue seem to say we will do no harm with our swords, and that Pyramus is not killed indeed; and for the more better assurance, tell them that I Pyramus am not Pyramus but Bottom the weaver. This will put them out of fear.

QUINCE.

Well, we will have such a prologue; and it shall be written in eight and six.

BOTTOM.

No, make it two more; let it be written in eight and eight.

SNOUT

Will not the ladies be afeard of the lion?

STARVELING.

I fear it, I promise you.

BOTTOM.

Masters, you ought to consider with yourselves, to bring in (God shield us!) a lion among ladies is a most dreadful thing. For there is not a more fearful wild-fowl than your lion living; and we ought to look to it.

SNOUT

Therefore another prologue must tell he is not a lion.

BOTTOM.

Nay, you must name his name, and half his face must be seen through the lion's neck; and he himself must speak through, saying thus, or to the same defect: 'Ladies,' or, 'Fair ladies, I would wish you,' or, 'I would request you,' or, 'I would entreat you, not to fear, not to tremble: my life for yours. If you think I come hither as a lion, it were pity of my life. No, I am no such thing; I am a man as other men are': and there, indeed, let him name his name, and tell them plainly he is Snug the joiner.

QUINCE.

Well, it shall be so. But there is two hard things: that is, to bring the moonlight into a chamber, for you know, Pyramus and Thisbe meet by moonlight.

SNOUT

Doth the moon shine that night we play our play?

BOTTOM.

A calendar, a calendar! Look in the almanack; find out moonshine, find out moonshine.

QUINCE.

Yes, it doth shine that night.

BOTTOM.

Why, then may you leave a casement of the great chamber window, where we play, open; and the moon may shine in at the casement.

QUINCE.

Ay; or else one must come in with a bush of thorns and a lantern, and say he comes to disfigure or to present the person of Moonshine. Then there is another thing: we must have a wall in the great chamber; for Pyramus and Thisbe, says the story, did talk through the chink of a wall.

SNOUT

You can never bring in a wall. What say you, Bottom?

BOTTOM.

Some man or other must present Wall. And let him have some plaster, or some loam, or some roughcast about him, to signify wall; and let him hold his fingers thus, and through that cranny shall Pyramus and Thisbe whisper.

QUINCE.

If that may be, then all is well. Come, sit down, every mother's son, and rehearse your parts. Pyramus, you begin: when you have spoken your speech, enter into that brake; and so everyone according to his cue.

Enter Puck behind.

PUCK.

What hempen homespuns have we swaggering here,

So near the cradle of the Fairy Queen?

What, a play toward? I'll be an auditor;

An actor too perhaps, if I see cause.

QUINCE.

Speak, Pyramus.—Thisbe, stand forth.

PYRAMUS.

Thisbe, the flowers of odious savours sweet

QUINCE.

Odours, odours.

PYRAMUS.

. . . odours savours sweet.

So hath thy breath, my dearest Thisbe dear.

But hark, a voice! Stay thou but here awhile,

And by and by I will to thee appear.

[Exit.]

PUCK.

A stranger Pyramus than e'er played here!

[Exit.]

THISBE.

Must I speak now?

QUINCE.

Ay, marry, must you, For you must understand he goes but to see a noise that he heard, and is to come again.

THISBE.

Most radiant Pyramus, most lily-white of hue,

Of colour like the red rose on triumphant brier,

Most brisky juvenal, and eke most lovely Jew,

As true as truest horse, that yet would never tire,

I'll meet thee, Pyramus, at Ninny's tomb.

QUINCE.

Ninus' tomb, man! Why, you must not speak that yet. That you answer to Pyramus. You speak all your part at once, cues, and all.—Pyramus enter! Your cue is past; it is 'never tire.'

THISBE.

O, As true as truest horse, that yet would never tire.

Enter Puck and Bottom with an ass's head.

PYRAMUS.

If I were fair, Thisbe, I were only thine.

QUINCE.

O monstrous! O strange! We are haunted. Pray, masters, fly, masters! Help!

[Exeunt Clowns.]

PUCK.

I'll follow you. I'll lead you about a round,

   Through bog, through bush, through brake, through brier;

Sometime a horse I'll be, sometime a hound,

   A hog, a headless bear, sometime a fire;

And neigh, and bark, and grunt, and roar, and burn,

Like horse, hound, hog, bear, fire, at every turn.

[Exit.]

BOTTOM.

Why do they run away? This is a knavery of them to make me afeard.

Enter Snout.

SNOUT

O Bottom, thou art changed! What do I see on thee?

BOTTOM.

What do you see? You see an ass-head of your own, do you?

[Exit Snout.]

Enter Quince.

QUINCE.

Bless thee, Bottom! bless thee! Thou art translated.

[Exit.]

BOTTOM.

I see their knavery. This is to make an ass of me, to fright me, if they could. But I will not stir from this place, do what they can. I will walk up and down here, and I will sing, that they shall hear I am not afraid.

Stage: 4   Topic: Categories Comedy, History and Tragedy
Lesson: 19

Learning Intention: Understanding the different categories of the plays: History.

Teaching strategy: Teacher directed notes and discussion with questions.

Presentation:
- Settle class and Roll.
- Hand out your chosen play script (You only need to use one of the three options provided.) and Read or watch play extract
- After watching give the students the following questions:

These questions can be answered as a class on the board or in pairs in their books and then bring the class back together to discuss their answers.
- What is happening?
- What techniques are being used?
- What makes it Comedy/ History/Tragedy?
- Do elements from other genres enter?
- How might the staging emphasise the genre?
- Pack up

Lesson reflection:

History Plays

Henry V

ACT IV SCENE III. The English camp.

Enter Gloucester, Bedford, Exeter, Erpingham, with all his host: Salisbury and Westmorland.

GLOUCESTER.

Where is the King?

BEDFORD.

The King himself is rode to view their battle.

WESTMORLAND.

Of fighting men they have full three-score thousand.

EXETER.

There's five to one; besides, they all are fresh.

SALISBURY.

God's arm strike with us! 'tis a fearful odds.

God be wi' you, princes all; I'll to my charge.

If we no more meet till we meet in heaven,

Then, joyfully, my noble Lord of Bedford,

My dear Lord Gloucester, and my good Lord Exeter,

And my kind kinsman, warriors all, adieu!

BEDFORD.

Farewell, good Salisbury, and good luck go with thee!

EXETER.

Farewell, kind lord; fight valiantly today!

And yet I do thee wrong to mind thee of it,

For thou art fram'd of the firm truth of valour.

[Exit Salisbury.]

BEDFORD.

He is as full of valour as of kindness,

Princely in both.

Enter the King.

WESTMORLAND.

O that we now had here

But one ten thousand of those men in England

That do no work today!

KING.

What's he that wishes so?

My cousin Westmorland? No, my fair cousin.

If we are mark'd to die, we are enough

To do our country loss; and if to live,

The fewer men, the greater share of honour.

God's will! I pray thee, wish not one man more.

By Jove, I am not covetous for gold,

Nor care I who doth feed upon my cost;

It yearns me not if men my garments wear;

Such outward things dwell not in my desires;

But if it be a sin to covet honour,

I am the most offending soul alive.

No, faith, my coz, wish not a man from England.

God's peace! I would not lose so great an honour

As one man more, methinks, would share from me

For the best hope I have. O, do not wish one more!

Rather proclaim it, Westmorland, through my host,

That he which hath no stomach to this fight,

Let him depart. His passport shall be made,

And crowns for convoy put into his purse.

We would not die in that man's company

That fears his fellowship to die with us.

This day is call'd the feast of Crispian.

He that outlives this day, and comes safe home,

Will stand a tip-toe when this day is named,

And rouse him at the name of Crispian.

He that shall live this day, and see old age,

Will yearly on the vigil feast his neighbours,

And say, "Tomorrow is Saint Crispian."

Then will he strip his sleeve and show his scars,

And say, "These wounds I had on Crispian's day."

Old men forget; yet all shall be forgot,

But he'll remember with advantages

What feats he did that day. Then shall our names,

Familiar in his mouth as household words,

Harry the King, Bedford, and Exeter,

Warwick and Talbot, Salisbury and Gloucester,

Be in their flowing cups freshly remembered.

This story shall the good man teach his son;

And Crispin Crispian shall ne'er go by,

From this day to the ending of the world,

But we in it shall be remembered,

We few, we happy few, we band of brothers.

For he today that sheds his blood with me

Shall be my brother; be he ne'er so vile,

This day shall gentle his condition;

And gentlemen in England now abed

Shall think themselves accurs'd they were not here,

And hold their manhoods cheap whiles any speaks

That fought with us upon Saint Crispin's day.

Enter Salisbury.

SALISBURY.

My sovereign lord, bestow yourself with speed.

The French are bravely in their battles set,

And will with all expedience charge on us.

KING HENRY.

All things are ready, if our minds be so.

WESTMORLAND.

Perish the man whose mind is backward now!

KING HENRY.

Thou dost not wish more help from England, coz?

WESTMORLAND.

God's will! my liege, would you and I alone,

Without more help, could fight this royal battle!

KING HENRY.

Why, now thou hast unwish'd five thousand men,

Which likes me better than to wish us one.

You know your places. God be with you all!

Tucket. Enter Montjoy.

MONTJOY.

Once more I come to know of thee, King Harry,

If for thy ransom thou wilt now compound,

Before thy most assured overthrow;

For certainly thou art so near the gulf,

Thou needs must be englutted. Besides, in mercy,

The Constable desires thee thou wilt mind

Thy followers of repentance; that their souls

May make a peaceful and a sweet retire

From off these fields, where, wretches, their poor bodies

Must lie and fester.

KING HENRY.

Who hath sent thee now?

MONTJOY.

The Constable of France.

KING HENRY.

I pray thee, bear my former answer back:

Bid them achieve me and then sell my bones.

Good God! why should they mock poor fellows thus?

The man that once did sell the lion's skin

While the beast liv'd, was kill'd with hunting him.

A many of our bodies shall no doubt

Find native graves, upon the which, I trust,

Shall witness live in brass of this day's work;

And those that leave their valiant bones in France,

Dying like men, though buried in your dunghills,

They shall be fam'd; for there the sun shall greet them,

And draw their honours reeking up to heaven;

Leaving their earthly parts to choke your clime,

The smell whereof shall breed a plague in France.

Mark then abounding valour in our English,

That being dead, like to the bullet's grazing,

Break out into a second course of mischief,

Killing in relapse of mortality.

Let me speak proudly: tell the Constable

We are but warriors for the working-day.

Our gayness and our gilt are all besmirch'd

With rainy marching in the painful field;

There's not a piece of feather in our host—

Good argument, I hope, we will not fly—

And time hath worn us into slovenry;

But, by the mass, our hearts are in the trim;

And my poor soldiers tell me, yet ere night

They'll be in fresher robes, or they will pluck

The gay new coats o'er the French soldiers' heads

And turn them out of service. If they do this—

As, if God please, they shall,—my ransom then

Will soon be levied. Herald, save thou thy labour.

Come thou no more for ransom, gentle herald.

They shall have none, I swear, but these my joints;

Which if they have as I will leave 'em them,

Shall yield them little, tell the Constable.

MONTJOY.

I shall, King Harry. And so fare thee well;

Thou never shalt hear herald any more.

Richard III

ACT I. SCENE I. London. A street

Enter RICHARD, DUKE OF GLOUCESTER, solus

GLOUCESTER.

Now is the winter of our discontent

Made glorious summer by this sun of York;

And all the clouds that lour'd upon our house

In the deep bosom of the ocean buried.

Now are our brows bound with victorious wreaths;

Our bruised arms hung up for monuments;

Our stern alarums chang'd to merry meetings,

Our dreadful marches to delightful measures.

Grim-visag'd war hath smooth'd his wrinkled front,

And now, instead of mounting barbed steeds

To fright the souls of fearful adversaries,

He capers nimbly in a lady's chamber

To the lascivious pleasing of a lute.

But I-that am not shap'd for sportive tricks,

Nor made to court an amorous looking-glass-

I-that am rudely stamp'd, and want love's majesty

To strut before a wanton ambling nymph-

I-that am curtail'd of this fair proportion,

Cheated of feature by dissembling nature,

Deform'd, unfinish'd, sent before my time

Into this breathing world scarce half made up,

And that so lamely and unfashionable

That dogs bark at me as I halt by them-

Why, I, in this weak piping time of peace,

Have no delight to pass away the time,

Unless to spy my shadow in the sun

And descant on mine own deformity.

And therefore, since I cannot prove a lover

To entertain these fair well-spoken days,

I am determined to prove a villain

And hate the idle pleasures of these days.

Plots have I laid, inductions dangerous,

By drunken prophecies, libels, and dreams,

To set my brother Clarence and the King

In deadly hate the one against the other;

And if King Edward be as true and just

As I am subtle, false, and treacherous,

This day should Clarence closely be mew'd up-

About a prophecy which says that G

Of Edward's heirs the murderer shall be.

Dive, thoughts, down to my soul. Here Clarence comes.

Enter CLARENCE, guarded, and BRAKENBURY

Brother, good day. What means this armed guard

That waits upon your Grace?

CLARENCE.

His Majesty,

Tend'ring my person's safety, hath appointed

This conduct to convey me to th' Tower.

GLOUCESTER.

Upon what cause?

CLARENCE.

Because my name is George.

GLOUCESTER.

Alack, my lord, that fault is none of yours:

He should, for that, commit your godfathers.

O, belike his Majesty hath some intent

That you should be new-christ'ned in the Tower.

But what's the matter, Clarence? May I know?

CLARENCE.

Yea, Richard, when I know; for I protest

As yet I do not; but, as I can learn,

He hearkens after prophecies and dreams,

And from the cross-row plucks the letter G,

And says a wizard told him that by G

His issue disinherited should be;

And, for my name of George begins with G,

It follows in his thought that I am he.

These, as I learn, and such like toys as these

Hath mov'd his Highness to commit me now.

GLOUCESTER.

Why, this it is when men are rul'd by women:

'Tis not the King that sends you to the Tower;

My Lady Grey his wife, Clarence, 'tis she

That tempers him to this extremity.

Was it not she and that good man of worship,

Antony Woodville, her brother there,

That made him send Lord Hastings to the Tower,

From whence this present day he is delivered?

We are not safe, Clarence; we are not safe.

CLARENCE.

By heaven, I think there is no man is secure

But the Queen's kindred, and night-walking heralds

That trudge betwixt the King and Mistress Shore.

Heard you not what an humble suppliant

Lord Hastings was, for her delivery?

GLOUCESTER.

Humbly complaining to her deity

Got my Lord Chamberlain his liberty.

I'll tell you what-I think it is our way,

If we will keep in favour with the King,

To be her men and wear her livery:

The jealous o'er-worn widow, and herself,

Since that our brother dubb'd them gentlewomen,

Are mighty gossips in our monarchy.

BRAKENBURY.

I beseech your Graces both to pardon me:

His Majesty hath straitly given in charge

That no man shall have private conference,

Of what degree soever, with your brother.

GLOUCESTER.

Even so; an't please your worship, Brakenbury,

You may partake of any thing we say:

We speak no treason, man; we say the King

Is wise and virtuous, and his noble queen

Well struck in years, fair, and not jealous;

We say that Shore's wife hath a pretty foot,

A cherry lip, a bonny eye, a passing pleasing tongue;

And that the Queen's kindred are made gentlefolks.

How say you, sir? Can you deny all this?

BRAKENBURY.

With this, my lord, myself have naught to do.

GLOUCESTER.

Naught to do with Mistress Shore! I tell thee,

fellow,

He that doth naught with her, excepting one,

Were best to do it secretly alone.

BRAKENBURY.

What one, my lord?

GLOUCESTER.

Her husband, knave! Wouldst thou betray me?

BRAKENBURY.

I do beseech your Grace to pardon me, and

withal

Forbear your conference with the noble Duke.

CLARENCE.

We know thy charge, Brakenbury, and will

obey.

GLOUCESTER.

We are the Queen's abjects and must obey.

Brother, farewell; I will unto the King;

And whatsoe'er you will employ me in-

Were it to call King Edward's widow sister-

I will perform it to enfranchise you.

Meantime, this deep disgrace in brotherhood

Touches me deeper than you can imagine.

CLARENCE.

I know it pleaseth neither of us well.

GLOUCESTER.

Well, your imprisonment shall not be long;

I will deliver or else lie for you.

Meantime, have patience.

CLARENCE.

I must perforce. Farewell.

            Exeunt CLARENCE, BRAKENBURY, and guard

Henry IV Part 1

ACT I SCENE III. The Same. A Room in the Palace.

HOTSPUR.

An if the Devil come and roar for them,

I will not send them: I will after straight,

And tell him so; for I will else my heart,

Although it be with hazard of my head.

NORTHUMBERLAND.

What, drunk with choler? stay, and pause awhile:

Here comes your uncle.

[Re-enter Worcester.]

HOTSPUR.

Speak of Mortimer!

Zounds, I will speak of him; and let my soul

Want mercy, if I do not join with him:

Yea, on his part I'll empty all these veins,

And shed my dear blood drop by drop i' the dust,

But I will lift the down-trod Mortimer

As high i' the air as this unthankful King,

As this ingrate and canker'd Bolingbroke.

NORTH.

[To Worcester.]

Brother, the King hath made your nephew mad.

WORCESTER.

Who struck this heat up after I was gone?

HOTSPUR.

He will, forsooth, have all my prisoners;

And when I urged the ransom once again

Of my wife's brother, then his cheek look'd pale,

And on my face he turn'd an eye of death,

Trembling even at the name of Mortimer.

WORCESTER.

I cannot blame him: was not he proclaim'd

By Richard that dead is the next of blood?

NORTHUMBERLAND.

He was; I heard the proclamation:

And then it was when the unhappy King—

Whose wrongs in us God pardon!—did set forth

Upon his Irish expedition;

From whence he intercepted did return

To be deposed, and shortly murdered.

WORCESTER.

And for whose death we in the world's wide mouth

Live scandalized and foully spoken of.

HOTSPUR.

But, soft! I pray you; did King Richard then

Proclaim my brother Edmund Mortimer

Heir to the crown?

NORTHUMBERLAND.

He did; myself did hear it.

HOTSPUR.

Nay, then I cannot blame his cousin King,

That wish'd him on the barren mountains starve.

But shall it be, that you, that set the crown

Upon the head of this forgetful man,

And for his sake wear the detested blot

Of murderous subornation,—shall it be,

That you a world of curses undergo,

Being the agents, or base second means,

The cords, the ladder, or the hangman rather?—

O, pardon me, that I descend so low,

To show the line and the predicament

Wherein you range under this subtle King;—

Shall it, for shame, be spoken in these days,

Or fill up chronicles in time to come,

That men of your nobility and power

Did gage them both in an unjust behalf,—

As both of you, God pardon it! have done,—

To put down Richard, that sweet lovely rose,

And plant this thorn, this canker, Bolingbroke?

And shall it, in more shame, be further spoken,

That you are fool'd, discarded, and shook off

By him for whom these shames ye underwent?

No! yet time serves, wherein you may redeem

Your banish'd honours, and restore yourselves

Into the good thoughts of the world again;

Revenge the jeering and disdain'd contempt

Of this proud King, who studies day and night

To answer all the debt he owes to you

Even with the bloody payment of your deaths:

Therefore, I say,—

WORCESTER.

Peace, cousin, say no more:

And now I will unclasp a secret book,

And to your quick-conceiving discontent

I'll read you matter deep and dangerous;

As full of peril and adventurous spirit

As to o'er-walk a current roaring loud

On the unsteadfast footing of a spear.

HOTSPUR.

If we fall in, good night, or sink or swim!

Send danger from the east unto the west,

So honour cross it from the north to south,

And let them grapple. O, the blood more stirs

To rouse a lion than to start a hare!

NORTHUMBERLAND.

Imagination of some great exploit

Drives him beyond the bounds of patience.

HOTSPUR.

By Heaven, methinks it were an easy leap,

To pluck bright honour from the pale-faced Moon;

Or dive into the bottom of the deep,

Where fathom-line could never touch the ground,

And pluck up drowned honour by the locks;

So he that doth redeem her thence might wear

Without corrival all her dignities:

But out upon this half-faced fellowship!

WORCESTER.

He apprehends a world of figures here,

But not the form of what he should attend.—

Good cousin, give me audience for a while.

HOTSPUR.

I cry you mercy.

WORCESTER.

Those same noble Scots

That are your prisoners,—

HOTSPUR.

I'll keep them all;

By God, he shall not have a Scot of them;

No, if a Scot would save his soul, he shall not:

I'll keep them, by this hand.

WORCESTER.

You start away,

And lend no ear unto my purposes.

Those prisoners you shall keep;—

HOTSPUR.

Nay, I will; that's flat.

He said he would not ransom Mortimer;

Forbade my tongue to speak of Mortimer;

But I will find him when he lies asleep,

And in his ear I'll holla Mortimer!

Nay,

I'll have a starling shall be taught to speak

Nothing but Mortimer, and give it him,

To keep his anger still in motion.

WORCESTER.

Hear you, cousin; a word.

HOTSPUR.

All studies here I solemnly defy,

Save how to gall and pinch this Bolingbroke:

And that same sword-and-buckler Prince of Wales,

But that I think his father loves him not,

And would be glad he met with some mischance,

I'd have him poison'd with a pot of ale.

WORCESTER.

Farewell, kinsman: I will talk to you

When you are better temper'd to attend.

NORTHUMBERLAND.

Why, what a wasp-stung and impatient fool

Art thou, to break into this woman's mood,

Tying thine ear to no tongue but thine own!

HOTSPUR.

Why, look you, I am whipp'd and scourged with rods,

Nettled, and stung with pismires, when I hear

Of this vile politician, Bolingbroke.

In Richard's time,—what do you call the place?—

A plague upon't!—it is in Gioucestershire;—

'Twas where the madcap Duke his uncle kept,

His uncle York;—where I first bow'd my knee

Unto this king of smiles, this Bolingbroke;—

When you and he came back from Ravenspurg.

NORTHUMBERLAND.

At Berkeley-castle.

HOTSPUR.

You say true:—

Why, what a candy deal of courtesy

This fawning greyhound then did proffer me!

Look, when his infant fortune came to age,

And, Gentle Harry Percy, and kind cousin,—

O, the Devil take such cozeners!—God forgive me!—

Good uncle, tell your tale; for I have done.

WORCESTER.

Nay, if you have not, to't again;

We'll stay your leisure.

HOTSPUR.

I have done, i'faith.

WORCESTER.

Then once more to your Scottish prisoners.

Deliver them up without their ransom straight,

And make the Douglas' son your only mean

For powers in Scotland; which, for divers reasons

Which I shall send you written, be assured,

Will easily be granted.—

[To Northumberland.] You, my lord,

Your son in Scotland being thus employ'd,

Shall secretly into the bosom creep

Of that same noble prelate, well beloved,

Th' Archbishop.

HOTSPUR.

Of York, is't not?

WORCESTER.

True; who bears hard

His brother's death at Bristol, the Lord Scroop.

I speak not this in estimation,

As what I think might be, but what I know

Is ruminated, plotted, and set down,

And only stays but to behold the face

Of that occasion that shall bring it on.

HOTSPUR.

I smell't: upon my life, it will do well.

NORTHUMBERLAND.

Before the game's a-foot, thou still lett'st slip.

HOTSPUR.

Why, it cannot choose but be a noble plot:—

And then the power of Scotland and of York

To join with Mortimer, ha?

WORCESTER.

And so they shall.

HOTSPUR.

In faith, it is exceedingly well aim'd.

WORCESTER.

And 'tis no little reason bids us speed,

To save our heads by raising of a head;

For, bear ourselves as even as we can,

The King will always think him in our debt,

And think we think ourselves unsatisfied,

Till he hath found a time to pay us home:

And see already how he doth begin

To make us strangers to his looks of love.

HOTSPUR.

He does, he does: we'll be revenged on him.

WORCESTER.

Cousin, farewell: no further go in this

Than I by letters shall direct your course.

When time is ripe,— which will be suddenly,—

I'll steal to Glendower and Lord Mortimer;

Where you and Douglas, and our powers at once,

As I will fashion it, shall happily meet,

To bear our fortunes in our own strong arms,

Which now we hold at much uncertainty.

NORTHUMBERLAND.

Farewell, good brother: we shall thrive, I trust.

HOTSPUR.

Uncle, adieu: O, let the hours be short,

Till fields and blows and groans applaud our sport!

[Exeunt.]

Stage: 4   Topic: Categories Comedy, History and Tragedy
Lesson: 20

Learning Intention: Understanding the different categories of the plays: Tragedy.

Teaching strategy: Teacher directed notes and discussion with questions.

Presentation:
- Settle class and Roll.
- Hand out your chosen play script (You only need to use one of the three options provided.) and Read or watch play extract
- After watching give the students the following questions:
These questions can be answered as a class on the board or in pairs in their books and then bring the class back together to discuss their answers.
- What is happening?
- What techniques are being used?
- What makes it Comedy/ History/Tragedy?
- Do elements from other genres enter?
- How might the staging emphasise the genre?
- Pack up

Lesson reflection:

Julius Caesar

ACT V SCENE III. Another part of the field.

Alarum. Enter Cassius and Titinius.

CASSIUS.

O, look, Titinius, look, the villains fly!

Myself have to mine own turn'd enemy:

This ensign here of mine was turning back;

I slew the coward, and did take it from him.

TITINIUS.

O Cassius, Brutus gave the word too early,

Who, having some advantage on Octavius,

Took it too eagerly: his soldiers fell to spoil,

Whilst we by Antony are all enclos'd.

Enter Pindarus.

PINDARUS.

Fly further off, my lord, fly further off;

Mark Antony is in your tents, my lord.

Fly, therefore, noble Cassius, fly far off.

CASSIUS.

This hill is far enough. Look, look, Titinius;

Are those my tents where I perceive the fire?

TITINIUS.

They are, my lord.

CASSIUS.

Titinius, if thou lovest me,

Mount thou my horse and hide thy spurs in him,

Till he have brought thee up to yonder troops

And here again, that I may rest assur'd

Whether yond troops are friend or enemy.

TITINIUS.

I will be here again, even with a thought.

[Exit.]

CASSIUS.

Go, Pindarus, get higher on that hill,

My sight was ever thick. Regard Titinius,

And tell me what thou notest about the field.

[Pindarus goes up.]

This day I breathed first. Time is come round,

And where I did begin, there shall I end.

My life is run his compass. Sirrah, what news?

PINDARUS.

[Above.] O my lord!

CASSIUS.

What news?

PINDARUS.

[Above.] Titinius is enclosed round about

With horsemen, that make to him on the spur,

Yet he spurs on. Now they are almost on him.

Now, Titinius! Now some light. O, he lights too.

He's ta'en!

[Shout.]

And, hark! they shout for joy.

CASSIUS.

Come down; behold no more.

O, coward that I am, to live so long,

To see my best friend ta'en before my face!

[Pindarus descends.]

Come hither, sirrah.

In Parthia did I take thee prisoner;

And then I swore thee, saving of thy life,

That whatsoever I did bid thee do,

Thou shouldst attempt it. Come now, keep thine oath.

Now be a freeman; and with this good sword,

That ran through Caesar's bowels, search this bosom.

Stand not to answer. Here, take thou the hilts;

And when my face is cover'd, as 'tis now,

Guide thou the sword.—Caesar, thou art reveng'd,

Even with the sword that kill'd thee.

[Dies.]

PINDARUS.

So, I am free, yet would not so have been,

Durst I have done my will. O Cassius!

Far from this country Pindarus shall run,

Where never Roman shall take note of him.

King Lear

ACT V SCENE III. The British Camp near Dover.

Enter Lear with Cordelia dead in his arms; Edgar, Officer and others following.

LEAR.

Howl, howl, howl, howl! O, you are men of stone.

Had I your tongues and eyes, I'd use them so

That heaven's vault should crack. She's gone for ever!

I know when one is dead, and when one lives;

She's dead as earth. Lend me a looking glass;

If that her breath will mist or stain the stone,

Why, then she lives.

KENT.

Is this the promis'd end?

EDGAR.

Or image of that horror?

ALBANY.

Fall, and cease!

LEAR.

This feather stirs; she lives! If it be so,

It is a chance which does redeem all sorrows

That ever I have felt.

KENT.

O, my good master! [Kneeling.]

LEAR.

Prythee, away!

EDGAR.

'Tis noble Kent, your friend.

LEAR.

A plague upon you, murderers, traitors all!

I might have sav'd her; now she's gone for ever!

Cordelia, Cordelia! stay a little. Ha!

What is't thou say'st? Her voice was ever soft,

Gentle, and low, an excellent thing in woman.

I kill'd the slave that was a-hanging thee.

OFFICER.

'Tis true, my lords, he did.

LEAR.

Did I not, fellow?

I have seen the day, with my good biting falchion

I would have made them skip. I am old now,

And these same crosses spoil me. Who are you?

Mine eyes are not o' the best, I'll tell you straight.

KENT.

If Fortune brag of two she lov'd and hated,

One of them we behold.

LEAR.

This is a dull sight. Are you not Kent?

KENT.

The same,

Your servant Kent. Where is your servant Caius?

LEAR.

He's a good fellow, I can tell you that;

He'll strike, and quickly too:. He's dead and rotten.

KENT.

No, my good lord; I am the very man.

LEAR.

I'll see that straight.

KENT.

That from your first of difference and decay

Have follow'd your sad steps.

LEAR.

You are welcome hither.

KENT.

Nor no man else. All's cheerless, dark and deadly.

Your eldest daughters have fordone themselves,

And desperately are dead.

LEAR.

Ay, so I think.

ALBANY.

He knows not what he says; and vain is it

That we present us to him.

EDGAR.

Very bootless.

Enter an Officer.

OFFICER.

Edmund is dead, my lord.

ALBANY.

That's but a trifle here.

You lords and noble friends, know our intent.

What comfort to this great decay may come

Shall be applied For us, we will resign,

During the life of this old majesty,

To him our absolute power;

[to Edgar and Kent] you to your rights;

With boot and such addition as your honours

Have more than merited. All friends shall taste

The wages of their virtue and all foes

The cup of their deservings. O, see, see!

LEAR.

And my poor fool is hang'd! No, no, no life!

Why should a dog, a horse, a rat have life,

And thou no breath at all? Thou'lt come no more,

Never, never, never, never, never!

Pray you undo this button. Thank you, sir.

Do you see this? Look on her: look, her lips,

Look there, look there!

[He dies.]

Macbeth

ACT V SCENE V. Dunsinane. Within the castle.

Enter with drum and colours, Macbeth, Seyton and Soldiers.

MACBETH.

Hang out our banners on the outward walls;

The cry is still, "They come!" Our castle's strength

Will laugh a siege to scorn: here let them lie

Till famine and the ague eat them up.

Were they not forc'd with those that should be ours,

We might have met them dareful, beard to beard,

And beat them backward home.

[A cry of women within.]

What is that noise?

SEYTON.

It is the cry of women, my good lord.

[Exit.]

MACBETH.

I have almost forgot the taste of fears.

The time has been, my senses would have cool'd

To hear a night-shriek; and my fell of hair

Would at a dismal treatise rouse and stir

As life were in't. I have supp'd full with horrors;

Direness, familiar to my slaughterous thoughts,

Cannot once start me.

Enter Seyton.

Wherefore was that cry?

SEYTON.

The Queen, my lord, is dead.

MACBETH.

She should have died hereafter.

There would have been a time for such a word.

Tomorrow, and tomorrow, and tomorrow,

Creeps in this petty pace from day to day,

To the last syllable of recorded time;

And all our yesterdays have lighted fools

The way to dusty death. Out, out, brief candle!

Life's but a walking shadow; a poor player,

That struts and frets his hour upon the stage,

And then is heard no more: it is a tale

Told by an idiot, full of sound and fury,

Signifying nothing.

Enter a Messenger.

Thou com'st to use thy tongue; thy story quickly.

MESSENGER.

Gracious my lord,

I should report that which I say I saw,

But know not how to do't.

MACBETH.

Well, say, sir.

MESSENGER.

As I did stand my watch upon the hill,

I look'd toward Birnam, and anon, methought,

The wood began to move.

MACBETH.

Liar, and slave!

MESSENGER.

Let me endure your wrath, if't be not so.

Within this three mile may you see it coming;

I say, a moving grove.

MACBETH.

If thou speak'st false,

Upon the next tree shalt thou hang alive,

Till famine cling thee: if thy speech be sooth,

I care not if thou dost for me as much.—

I pull in resolution; and begin

To doubt th' equivocation of the fiend,

That lies like truth. "Fear not, till Birnam wood

Do come to Dunsinane;" and now a wood

Comes toward Dunsinane.—Arm, arm, and out!—

If this which he avouches does appear,

There is nor flying hence nor tarrying here.

I 'gin to be aweary of the sun,

And wish th' estate o' th' world were now undone.—

Ring the alarum bell!—Blow, wind! come, wrack!

At least we'll die with harness on our back.

Stage: 4   Topic: Types of Speech   Lesson: 21

Learning Intention: Looking at the different types of Speech used in Shakespeare's plays: Dialogue, Soliloquy and Speech

Teaching strategy: Teacher directed notes and discussion with questions.

Presentation:
- Settle class and Roll.
- Class notes on the types of speech used in Shakespeare.
- Look at examples of each. What do you notice about them?
- Why do you think Shakespeare stops his plays action to speak to the audience in soliloquies?
- Look at the speeches. What kinds of leaders are making these speeches? Do they advance the action? How are they different from the soliloquies?

These questions are best answered as a class on the board and recorded in their books.
- Pack up

Lesson reflection:

Types of speech.

Shakespeare's plays have three distinct styles of speech. Dialogue, where two or more characters are speaking together. Monologue, or soliloquy, where a character talks to themselves, without being heard by the other characters. And speeches, which like soliloquies are a solo character talking, but are addressed to everyone on stage as well as the audience.

Dialogue – this is the most common form of speech in a play. Its purpose is to allow the characters to exchange information, argue, fall in love, etc and to move the action forward. Scenes heavy in dialogue are what move the action of the play forward. Even duels and battle scenes contain dialogue to move the battle forward and show the antagonism between the opponents.

Soliloquy – This is a form of speech which stops the action as the character reflects on what is happening or what they plan to do. Richard III explains all his plots to the audience in soliloquies, which create an intimacy between him and the audience. We know what he is planning to do, and are either with him or increasingly horrified at the lengths to which he is willing to go to hold power. Hamlet too is famous for his long and frequent soliloquies, where he debates the course of action he will take. Not every character gets a soliloquy, they are generally reserved for major characters only.

Speech – Not to be confused with a Soliloquy, a speech is a persuasive form of speaking, and does help to drive the action forward. Speeches are mostly found in the History plays, in the mouths of kings, queens or heroes. These are designed to excite both the characters on the stage and the audience.

Examples of Dialogue:

from Henry VI Part 3

LEWIS.
Then, England's messenger, return in post
And tell false Edward, thy supposed king,
That Lewis of France is sending over masquers
To revel it with him and his new bride.
Thou seest what's past; go fear thy king withal.
BONA.
Tell him, in hope he'll prove a widower shortly,
I'll wear the willow-garland for his sake.
QUEEN MARGARET.
Tell him my mourning weeds are laid aside,
And I am ready to put armour on.
WARWICK.
Tell him from me that he hath done me wrong,
And therefore I'll uncrown him ere't be long.
There's thy reward; be gone.
Exit POST

From Hamlet:

HAMLET.
Beggar that I am, I am even poor in thanks; but I thank you. And sure, dear friends, my thanks are too dear a halfpenny. Were you not sent for? Is it your own inclining? Is it a free visitation? Come, deal justly with me. Come, come; nay, speak.
GUILDENSTERN.
What should we say, my lord?
HAMLET.
Why, anything. But to the purpose. You were sent for; and there is a kind of confession in your looks, which your modesties have not craft enough to colour. I know the good King and Queen have sent for you.
ROSENCRANTZ.
To what end, my lord?
HAMLET.
That you must teach me. But let me conjure you, by the rights of our fellowship, by the consonancy of our youth, by the obligation of our ever-preserved love, and by what more dear a better proposer could charge you withal, be even and direct with me, whether you were sent for or no.
ROSENCRANTZ.
[To Guildenstern.] What say you?
HAMLET.
[Aside.] Nay, then I have an eye of you. If you love me, hold not off.
GUILDENSTERN.
My lord, we were sent for.
HAMLET.
I will tell you why; so shall my anticipation prevent your discovery, and your secrecy to the King and Queen moult no feather. I have of late, but wherefore I know not, lost all my mirth, forgone all custom of exercises; and indeed, it goes so heavily with my disposition that this goodly frame the earth, seems to me a sterile promontory; this most excellent canopy the air, look you, this brave o'erhanging firmament, this majestical roof fretted with golden fire, why, it appears no other thing to me than a foul and pestilent congregation of vapours. What a piece of work is man! How noble in reason? How infinite in faculties, in form and moving, how express and admirable? In action how like an angel? In apprehension, how like a god? The beauty of the world, the paragon of animals. And yet, to me, what is this quintessence of dust? Man delights not me; no, nor woman neither, though by your smiling you seem to say so.
ROSENCRANTZ.
My lord, there was no such stuff in my thoughts.
HAMLET.
Why did you laugh then, when I said 'Man delights not me'?
ROSENCRANTZ.
To think, my lord, if you delight not in man, what Lenten entertainment the players shall receive from you. We coted them on the way, and hither are they coming to offer you service.

From Henry IV Part 1 a dialogue that ends in a soliloquy:

PRINCE.
Why, thou owest God a death.
[Exit.]
FALSTAFF.
'Tis not due yet; I would be loth to pay Him before His day. What need I be so forward with him that calls not on me? Well, 'tis no matter; honour pricks me on. Yea, but how if honour prick me off when I come on? how then? Can honor set-to a leg? no: or an arm? no: or take away the grief of a wound? no. Honour hath no skill in surgery then? no. What is honour? a word. What is that word, honour? air. A trim reckoning!—Who hath it? he that died o' Wednesday. Doth he feel it? no. Doth be hear it? no. Is it insensible, then? yea, to the dead. But will it not live with the living? no. Why? detraction will not suffer it. Therefore I'll none of it: honour is a mere scutcheon:—and so ends my catechism.
[Exit.]

Examples of Soliloquies:

From Macbeth

LADY MACBETH.
"They met me in the day of success; and I have learned by the perfect'st report they have more in them than mortal knowledge. When I burned in desire to question them further, they made themselves air, into which they vanished. Whiles I stood rapt in the wonder of it, came missives from the King, who all-hailed me, 'Thane of Cawdor'; by which title, before, these Weird Sisters saluted me, and referred me to the coming on of time, with 'Hail, king that shalt be!' This have I thought good to deliver thee (my dearest partner of greatness) that thou might'st not lose the dues of rejoicing, by being ignorant of what greatness is promis'd thee. Lay it to thy heart, and farewell."
Glamis thou art, and Cawdor; and shalt be
What thou art promis'd. Yet do I fear thy nature;
It is too full o' th' milk of human kindness
To catch the nearest way. Thou wouldst be great;
Art not without ambition, but without
The illness should attend it. What thou wouldst highly,
That wouldst thou holily; wouldst not play false,
And yet wouldst wrongly win. Thou'dst have, great Glamis,
That which cries, "Thus thou must do," if thou have it;
And that which rather thou dost fear to do,
Than wishest should be undone. Hie thee hither,
That I may pour my spirits in thine ear,
And chastise with the valour of my tongue
All that impedes thee from the golden round,
Which fate and metaphysical aid doth seem
To have thee crown'd withal.

From Hamlet

HAMLET.
Ay, so, God b' wi' ye. Now I am alone.
O what a rogue and peasant slave am I!
Is it not monstrous that this player here,
But in a fiction, in a dream of passion,
Could force his soul so to his own conceit
That from her working all his visage wan'd;
Tears in his eyes, distraction in's aspect,
A broken voice, and his whole function suiting
With forms to his conceit? And all for nothing!
For Hecuba?
What's Hecuba to him, or he to Hecuba,
That he should weep for her? What would he do,
Had he the motive and the cue for passion
That I have? He would drown the stage with tears
And cleave the general ear with horrid speech;
Make mad the guilty, and appal the free,
Confound the ignorant, and amaze indeed,
The very faculties of eyes and ears. Yet I,
A dull and muddy-mettled rascal, peak
Like John-a-dreams, unpregnant of my cause,
And can say nothing. No, not for a king
Upon whose property and most dear life
A damn'd defeat was made. Am I a coward?
Who calls me villain, breaks my pate across?
Plucks off my beard and blows it in my face?
Tweaks me by the nose, gives me the lie i' th' throat
As deep as to the lungs? Who does me this?
Ha! 'Swounds, I should take it: for it cannot be
But I am pigeon-liver'd, and lack gall
To make oppression bitter, or ere this
I should have fatted all the region kites
With this slave's offal. Bloody, bawdy villain!
Remorseless, treacherous, lecherous, kindless villain!
Oh vengeance!
Why, what an ass am I! This is most brave,
That I, the son of a dear father murder'd,
Prompted to my revenge by heaven and hell,
Must, like a whore, unpack my heart with words
And fall a-cursing like a very drab,
A scullion! Fie upon't! Foh!
About, my brain! I have heard
That guilty creatures sitting at a play,
Have by the very cunning of the scene,
Been struck so to the soul that presently
They have proclaim'd their malefactions.
For murder, though it have no tongue, will speak

With most miraculous organ. I'll have these players
Play something like the murder of my father
Before mine uncle. I'll observe his looks;
I'll tent him to the quick. If he but blench,
I know my course. The spirit that I have seen
May be the devil, and the devil hath power
T'assume a pleasing shape, yea, and perhaps
Out of my weakness and my melancholy,
As he is very potent with such spirits,
Abuses me to damn me. I'll have grounds
More relative than this. The play's the thing
Wherein I'll catch the conscience of the King.

Examples of speeches:

From Henry V

KING HENRY.
Once more unto the breach, dear friends, once more,
Or close the wall up with our English dead.
In peace there's nothing so becomes a man
As modest stillness and humility;
But when the blast of war blows in our ears,
Then imitate the action of the tiger;
Stiffen the sinews, summon up the blood,
Disguise fair nature with hard-favour'd rage;
Then lend the eye a terrible aspect;
Let it pry through the portage of the head
Like the brass cannon; let the brow o'erwhelm it
As fearfully as does a galled rock
O'erhang and jutty his confounded base,
Swill'd with the wild and wasteful ocean.
Now set the teeth and stretch the nostril wide,
Hold hard the breath, and bend up every spirit
To his full height. On, on, you noblest English,
Whose blood is fet from fathers of war-proof!
Fathers that, like so many Alexanders,
Have in these parts from morn till even fought,
And sheath'd their swords for lack of argument.
Dishonour not your mothers; now attest
That those whom you call'd fathers did beget you.
Be copy now to men of grosser blood,
And teach them how to war. And you, good yeomen,
Whose limbs were made in England, show us here
The mettle of your pasture; let us swear
That you are worth your breeding, which I doubt not;
For there is none of you so mean and base,
That hath not noble lustre in your eyes.

I see you stand like greyhounds in the slips,
Straining upon the start. The game's afoot!
Follow your spirit, and upon this charge
Cry, "God for Harry! England and Saint George!"

from Coriolanus

MARCIUS. All the contagion of the south light on you,
You shames of Rome! you herd of - Boils and plagues
Plaster you o'er, that you may be abhorr'd
Farther than seen, and one infect another
Against the wind a mile! You souls of geese
That bear the shapes of men, how have you run
From slaves that apes would beat! Pluto and hell!
All hurt behind! Backs red, and faces pale
With flight and agued fear! Mend and charge home,
Or, by the fires of heaven, I'll leave the foe
And make my wars on you. Look to't. Come on;
If you'll stand fast we'll beat them to their wives,
As they us to our trenches. Follow me.
Another alarum. The Volsces fly, and MARCIUS follows them to the gates
So, now the gates are ope; now prove good seconds;
'Tis for the followers fortune widens them,
Not for the fliers. Mark me, and do the like.

Stage: 4   Topic: Persuading the audience – Julius Caesar
Lesson: 22

Learning Intention: Comparing and contrasting two persuasive texts and how Shakespeare used rhetoric to build two different sides to his argument.

Teaching strategy: Teacher directed notes and discussion with questions.

Presentation:
- Settle class and Roll.
- Introduce the concept of rhetoric- arguing a point to persuade an audience
- Introduce Julius Caesar then watch Brutus' Speech justifying the assassination with students following on with the extract.
- What is happening?
- What rhetorical techniques are being used?
- Is Brutus' language persuasive? Why?

These questions are best answered as a class on the board and recorded in their books.
- Pack up

Lesson reflection:

Rhetorical language.

Rhetoric is the art of persuasion. It is a style of persuasive language that originates in Ancient Greece and Rome. During Shakespeare's time it was a skill taught in school. Boys would be taught not only to persuade an audience, but also to critically analyse the arguments of their opponents in order to understand and reply effectively. Rhetoric for the Elizabethan's did not just include the words said, but tone of voice, the way the speaker held their body and the way they used hand gestures.

An effective rhetorical speaker constructs a speech thinking about the following:

Audience – who are you speaking to and how do you want them to respond to what you are saying.

Self presentation, emotion and pleasure – The speaker must think about how they present themselves to their audience. What are the emotions that they wish to arouse in their audience and how best to draw them out. And finally, pleasure, how to keep the audience interested and listening to what you are saying. If the audience grows bored and restless they will not pay attention to your words.

Disposition and Structure – in what order are you making your arguments and revealing information.

Argument and narrative – How is the speaker taking the audience on a journey with them? How is the speaker building a story with their words? How are they employing logical arguments, emotive arguments and why are they in a position to say anything at all?

Character and description – The speaker must present an appealing character to the audience. In Coriolanus, the plebeians are turned against Coriolanus, when it is pointed out to them that his demeanour was offhand and haughty, rather than appearing humble. Note appearing, the speaker does not actually have to be any particular thing, they just need to seem it. Description involves verbal drawing of detailed images, something which runs across all of Shakespeare's writings.

Brutus' Speech Julius Caesar

Our first speech comes after the assassination of Caesar. Brutus and the other conspirators enter the forum to explain to the alarmed crowd why they have killed the most powerful man in the world. Brutus and the others enter waving their bloodied daggers, with their arms covered in Caesar's blood up to the elbows.

SCENE II. The same. The Forum.

Enter Brutus and goes into the pulpit, and Cassius, with a throng of Citizens.

CITIZENS.

We will be satisfied; let us be satisfied.

BRUTUS.

Then follow me, and give me audience, friends.

Cassius, go you into the other street

And part the numbers.

Those that will hear me speak, let 'em stay here;

Those that will follow Cassius, go with him;

And public reasons shall be rendered

Of Caesar's death.

FIRST CITIZEN.

I will hear Brutus speak.

SECOND CITIZEN.

I will hear Cassius; and compare their reasons,

When severally we hear them rendered.

[Exit Cassius, with some of the Citizens. Brutus goes into the rostrum.]

THIRD CITIZEN.

The noble Brutus is ascended: silence!

BRUTUS.

Be patient till the last.

Romans, countrymen, and lovers, hear me for my cause; and be silent, that you may hear. Believe me for mine honour, and have respect to mine honour, that you may believe. Censure me in your wisdom, and awake your senses, that you may the better judge. If there be any in this assembly, any dear friend of Caesar's, to him I say that Brutus' love to Caesar was no less than his. If then that friend demand why

Brutus rose against Caesar, this is my answer: Not that I loved Caesar less, but that I loved Rome more. Had you rather Caesar were living, and die all slaves, than that Caesar were dead, to live all free men? As Caesar loved me, I weep for him; as he was fortunate, I rejoice at it; as he was valiant, I honour him; but, as he was ambitious, I slew him. There is tears, for his love; joy for his fortune; honour for his valour; and death, for his ambition. Who is here so base, that would be a bondman? If any, speak; for him have I offended. Who is here so rude, that would not be a Roman? If any, speak; for him have I offended. Who is here so vile, that will not love his country? If any, speak; for him have I offended. I pause for a reply.

CITIZENS.

None, Brutus, none.

BRUTUS.

Then none have I offended. I have done no more to Caesar than you shall do to Brutus. The question of his death is enroll'd in the Capitol, his glory not extenuated, wherein he was worthy; nor his offences enforc'd, for which he suffered death.

Stage: 4 **Topic: Persuading the audience – Julius Caesar**
Lesson: 23

Learning Intention: Comparing and contrasting two persuasive texts and how Shakespeare used rhetoric to build two different sides to his argument.

Teaching strategy: Teacher directed notes and discussion with questions.

Presentation:
- Settle class and Roll.
- Introduce Julius Caesar then watch Antony's Speech condemning the assassination with students following on with the extract.
- What is happening?
- What rhetorical techniques are being used?
- Is Antony's language persuasive? Why?

These questions are best answered as a class on the board and recorded in their books.
- Pack up

Lesson reflection:

Antony's speech Julius Caesar's

Marc Antony is a powerful general and ally of Caesar, he has been given permission to speak after the conspirators, on the understanding that he will not condemn their actions. Not all of the conspirators are comfortable with this as Antony is known as a great speaker and they worry that he will sway the crowd against them.

ANTONY.

Friends, Romans, countrymen, lend me your ears;

I come to bury Caesar, not to praise him.

The evil that men do lives after them,

The good is oft interred with their bones;

So let it be with Caesar. The noble Brutus

Hath told you Caesar was ambitious.

If it were so, it was a grievous fault,

And grievously hath Caesar answer'd it.

Here, under leave of Brutus and the rest,

For Brutus is an honourable man,

So are they all, all honourable men,

Come I to speak in Caesar's funeral.

He was my friend, faithful and just to me;

But Brutus says he was ambitious,

And Brutus is an honourable man.

He hath brought many captives home to Rome,

Whose ransoms did the general coffers fill:

Did this in Caesar seem ambitious?

When that the poor have cried, Caesar hath wept;

Ambition should be made of sterner stuff:

Yet Brutus says he was ambitious;

And Brutus is an honourable man.

You all did see that on the Lupercal

I thrice presented him a kingly crown,

Which he did thrice refuse. Was this ambition?

Yet Brutus says he was ambitious;

And sure he is an honourable man.

I speak not to disprove what Brutus spoke,

But here I am to speak what I do know.

You all did love him once, not without cause;

What cause withholds you then to mourn for him?

O judgment, thou art fled to brutish beasts,

And men have lost their reason. Bear with me.

My heart is in the coffin there with Caesar,

And I must pause till it come back to me.

FIRST CITIZEN.

Methinks there is much reason in his sayings.

SECOND CITIZEN.

If thou consider rightly of the matter,

Caesar has had great wrong.

THIRD CITIZEN.

Has he, masters?

I fear there will a worse come in his place.

FOURTH CITIZEN.

Mark'd ye his words? He would not take the crown;

Therefore 'tis certain he was not ambitious.

FIRST CITIZEN.

If it be found so, some will dear abide it.

SECOND CITIZEN.

Poor soul, his eyes are red as fire with weeping.

THIRD CITIZEN.

There's not a nobler man in Rome than Antony.

FOURTH CITIZEN.

Now mark him; he begins again to speak.

ANTONY.

But yesterday the word of Caesar might

Have stood against the world; now lies he there,

And none so poor to do him reverence.

O masters! If I were dispos'd to stir

Your hearts and minds to mutiny and rage,

I should do Brutus wrong and Cassius wrong,

Who, you all know, are honourable men.

I will not do them wrong; I rather choose

To wrong the dead, to wrong myself and you,

Than I will wrong such honourable men.

But here's a parchment with the seal of Caesar,

I found it in his closet; 'tis his will:

Let but the commons hear this testament,

Which, pardon me, I do not mean to read,

And they would go and kiss dead Caesar's wounds,

And dip their napkins in his sacred blood;

Yea, beg a hair of him for memory,

And, dying, mention it within their wills,

Bequeathing it as a rich legacy

Unto their issue.

FOURTH CITIZEN.

We'll hear the will. Read it, Mark Antony.

CITIZENS.

The will, the will! We will hear Caesar's will.

ANTONY.

Have patience, gentle friends, I must not read it.

It is not meet you know how Caesar loved you.

You are not wood, you are not stones, but men;

And being men, hearing the will of Caesar,

It will inflame you, it will make you mad.

'Tis good you know not that you are his heirs;

For if you should, O, what would come of it?

FOURTH CITIZEN.

Read the will! We'll hear it, Antony;

You shall read us the will, Caesar's will!

ANTONY.

Will you be patient? Will you stay awhile?

I have o'ershot myself to tell you of it.

I fear I wrong the honourable men

Whose daggers have stabb'd Caesar; I do fear it.

FOURTH CITIZEN.

They were traitors. Honourable men!

CITIZENS.

The will! The testament!

SECOND CITIZEN.

They were villains, murderers. The will! Read the will!

ANTONY.

You will compel me then to read the will?

Then make a ring about the corpse of Caesar,

And let me show you him that made the will.

Shall I descend? and will you give me leave?

CITIZENS.

Come down.

SECOND CITIZEN.

Descend.

[He comes down.]

THIRD CITIZEN.

You shall have leave.

FOURTH CITIZEN.

A ring! Stand round.

FIRST CITIZEN.

Stand from the hearse, stand from the body.

SECOND CITIZEN.

Room for Antony, most noble Antony!

ANTONY.

Nay, press not so upon me; stand far off.

CITIZENS.

Stand back; room! bear back.

ANTONY.

If you have tears, prepare to shed them now.

You all do know this mantle. I remember

The first time ever Caesar put it on;

'Twas on a Summer's evening, in his tent,

That day he overcame the Nervii.

Look, in this place ran Cassius' dagger through:

See what a rent the envious Casca made:

Through this the well-beloved Brutus stabb'd;

And as he pluck'd his cursed steel away,

Mark how the blood of Caesar follow'd it,

As rushing out of doors, to be resolv'd

If Brutus so unkindly knock'd, or no;

For Brutus, as you know, was Caesar's angel.

Judge, O you gods, how dearly Caesar lov'd him.

This was the most unkindest cut of all;

For when the noble Caesar saw him stab,

Ingratitude, more strong than traitors' arms,

Quite vanquish'd him: then burst his mighty heart;

And in his mantle muffling up his face,

Even at the base of Pompey's statue

Which all the while ran blood, great Caesar fell.

O, what a fall was there, my countrymen!

Then I, and you, and all of us fell down,

Whilst bloody treason flourish'd over us.

O, now you weep; and I perceive you feel

The dint of pity. These are gracious drops.

Kind souls, what weep you when you but behold

Our Caesar's vesture wounded? Look you here,

Here is himself, marr'd, as you see, with traitors.

FIRST CITIZEN.

O piteous spectacle!

SECOND CITIZEN.

O noble Caesar!

THIRD CITIZEN.

O woeful day!

FOURTH CITIZEN.

O traitors, villains!

FIRST CITIZEN.

O most bloody sight!

SECOND CITIZEN.

We will be revenged.

CITIZENS.

Revenge,—about,—seek,—burn,—fire,—kill,—slay,—let not a traitor live!

ANTONY.

Stay, countrymen.

FIRST CITIZEN.

Peace there! Hear the noble Antony.

SECOND CITIZEN.

We'll hear him, we'll follow him, we'll die with him.

ANTONY.

Good friends, sweet friends, let me not stir you up

To such a sudden flood of mutiny.

They that have done this deed are honourable.

What private griefs they have, alas, I know not,

That made them do it. They're wise and honourable,

And will, no doubt, with reasons answer you.

I come not, friends, to steal away your hearts.

I am no orator, as Brutus is;

But, as you know me all, a plain blunt man,

That love my friend; and that they know full well

That gave me public leave to speak of him.

For I have neither wit, nor words, nor worth,

Action, nor utterance, nor the power of speech,

To stir men's blood. I only speak right on.

I tell you that which you yourselves do know,

Show you sweet Caesar's wounds, poor poor dumb mouths,

And bid them speak for me. But were I Brutus,

And Brutus Antony, there were an Antony

Would ruffle up your spirits, and put a tongue

In every wound of Caesar, that should move

The stones of Rome to rise and mutiny.

CITIZENS.

We'll mutiny.

FIRST CITIZEN.

We'll burn the house of Brutus.

THIRD CITIZEN.

Away, then! come, seek the conspirators.

ANTONY.

Yet hear me, countrymen; yet hear me speak.

CITIZENS.

Peace, ho! Hear Antony; most noble Antony.

ANTONY.

Why, friends, you go to do you know not what.

Wherein hath Caesar thus deserved your loves?

Alas, you know not; I must tell you then.

You have forgot the will I told you of.

CITIZENS.

Most true; the will!—let's stay, and hear the will.

ANTONY.

Here is the will, and under Caesar's seal.

To every Roman citizen he gives,

To every several man, seventy-five drachmas.

SECOND CITIZEN.

Most noble Caesar! We'll revenge his death.

THIRD CITIZEN.

O, royal Caesar!

ANTONY.

Hear me with patience.

CITIZENS.

Peace, ho!

ANTONY.

Moreover, he hath left you all his walks,

His private arbors, and new-planted orchards,

On this side Tiber; he hath left them you,

And to your heirs forever; common pleasures,

To walk abroad, and recreate yourselves.

Here was a Caesar! when comes such another?

FIRST CITIZEN.

Never, never. Come, away, away!

We'll burn his body in the holy place,

And with the brands fire the traitors' houses.

Take up the body.

SECOND CITIZEN.

Go, fetch fire.

THIRD CITIZEN.

Pluck down benches.

FOURTH CITIZEN.

Pluck down forms, windows, anything.

Stage: 4   **Topic: Persuading the audience – Julius Caesar**
Lesson: 24

Learning Intention: Comparing and contrasting two persuasive texts and how Shakespeare used rhetoric to build two different sides to his argument.

Teaching strategy: Teacher directed notes and discussion with questions.

Presentation:
- Settle class and Roll.
- Re-watch watch Brutus' Speech justifying the assassination followed by Antony's Speech condemning it with students following on with the extracts
- Why is Antony's speech stronger in the end?
- What do the different styles tell you about the two men?
- Who do you think will ultimately be victorious at the end of the play? Why?
- What does it tell you about the view of the Mob? Are they sympathetic or just easily led sheep?
- What does it tell you about the power of language?

These questions are best answered as a class on the board and recorded in their books.

Ask students to write down the names of five people in the class they would be happy/willing to work with in a group. You can then take this to help to create the groups for the next lesson.

- Pack up

Lesson reflection:

Stage: 4   Topic: Shakespeare Board Game   Lesson: 25 - 30

Learning Intention: Synthesise the learning of the unit into a board or card game.

Teaching strategy: Teacher directed instructions and group work
Presentation:
- Settle class and Roll.
- Introduce the assignment. Organise the class into groups of up to 5, and yes all students need to be in a group.
- Supervise group work.
- Students present the game to the class in the final lesson.
-Pack up
Lesson reflection:

Shakespeare board game – Survive Literary London

The Australian Curriculum outcomes:
• Create literary texts that draw upon text structures and language features of other texts for particular purposes and effects
• Share, reflect on, clarify and evaluate opinions and arguments about aspects of literary texts
• Apply increasing knowledge of vocabulary, text structures and language features to understand the content of texts *

The Task:
Each group will produce a board or card game for 2-5 players.
The game must have clearly defined instructions, rules, and objectives.
The game must include appropriate graphics and decorative elements.
The game must include at least TEN things that you have learnt about Shakespeare and Literary London during this unit.
Your game must refer to at least FIVE plays.
Your game must include at least EIGHT quotes from the play excerpts we have looked at.

By the end of the week each group will have produced:
- a game board or cards with all components required to play the game.
- a set of instructions and rules to play the game.
Each individual will produce:
- a reflection sheet explaining why you made the game the way you did, and how you found the process including the process of working in the group.

Success criteria:

Your game will be marked on how well you:
• Included relevant information from the unit into your game.
• Created a functional and well structured game.
• The clarity of your rules and instructions.
• How well you matched your visual elements to the content of the game.
• Explain the rational behind your game in the reflection sheet.
• How well you communicated with each other and worked as a group.
• Present your game to the class.

*© Australian Curriculum, Assessment and Reporting Authority (ACARA) 2010 to present, unless Otherwise indicated. This material was downloaded from the Australian Curriculum website (www.australiancurriculum.edu.au) (Website) (accessed 13 April 2023) and [was][was not] modified. The material is licensed under CC BY 4.0 (https://creativecommons.org/licenses/by/4.0). Version updates are tracked in the 'Curriculum version history' section on the 'About the Australian Curriculum' page (http://australiancurriculum.edu.au/about-the-australian-curriculum/) of the Australian Curriculum website.
ACARA does not endorse any product that uses the Australian Curriculum or make any representations as to the quality of such products. Any product that uses material

published on this website should not be taken to be affiliated with ACARA or have the sponsorship or approval of ACARA. It is up to each person to make their own assessment of the product, taking into account matters including, but not limited to, the version number and the degree to which the materials align with the content descriptions and achievement standards (where relevant). Where there is a claim of alignment, it is important to check that the materials align with the content descriptions and achievement standards (endorsed by all education Ministers), not the elaborations (examples provided by ACARA).

Marking Criteria:

35-29 Exceptional -
- Has included significantly more than the specified units of course material in their project, content choice reflects the theme of the game.
- The game is sophisticated, and has an over arching theme to draw it together.
- Rules and instructions are clear and easy to follow.
- Visual elements are complete, consistent with the theme and creatively executed.
- Rational behind the game is clearly communicated, and well thought out.
- Group communication was excellent, group needed no reminders to return to task, did not have disputes and had good time management.
- Presentation is engaging, clear and well planned, all students take part in the presenting.

28–22 Accomplished -
- Has included a little more than the specified units of course material in their project, content choice begins to tie into the theme of the game.
- The game is sophisticated, and has an over arching theme to draw it together.
- Rules and instructions are clear and easy to follow.
- Visual elements are complete, consistent with the theme and creatively executed.
- Rational behind the game is clearly communicated, and well thought out.
- Group communication was good, group needed occasional reminders to return to task, but did not have disputes and had good time management.
- Presentation is well planned, and clearly communicates the objective of the game. Most of the students contribute to the presentation.

21-15 Proficient -
- Has included specified units of course material in their project, there is consistency in content choice.
- The game is basic, but has an over arching theme to draw it together.
- Rules and instructions are clear and easy to follow.
- Visual elements are complete, consistent with the theme and well executed.
- Rational behind the game is clearly communicated, and well thought out.
- Group communication was fair, group needed occasional reminders to return to task, but resolved disputes amicably and had good time management.
- Presentation is basic and rapid, only some of the students speak.

14-8 Developing -
- Has included specified units of course material in their project, but there is no consistency in content choice.
- The game is basic and has no over arching theme to draw it together.
- Rules and instructions are too simple or too difficult to follow.

- Visual elements are incomplete, inconsistent with the theme or irrelevant.
- Rational behind the game is basically communicated, and poorly thought out.
- Group communication was satisfactory, group did need reminders to return to task, but had no major disputes and had poor time management.
- Presentation is ad-libed and confusing. Only one speaker.

7-0 Elementary -
- Has not included specified units of course material in their project.
- The game lacks coherence or structure and is incomplete.
- Rules and instructions are missing, confusing or incomplete.
- Visual elements are incomplete, missing or irrelevant.
- Rational behind the game is poorly communicated, vague, incoherent or incomplete.
- Group communication was poor, disputes derailed the activity and had to be mediated by teacher, group did not use the class time well and disrupted other students.
- Presentation is not performed.

Score   /35

Henry IV Part 1

Year 10 Unit.

Stage: 5 **Topic: Introduction to Henry IV Part** **Lesson: 1**

Learning Intention: Students have an introduction to the play studied and understand the genre of play.

Teaching strategy: Explicit teacher centred instruction.
Presentation:
- Settle class and Roll.
- What is a history play? Class notes
- Talk with the students about why they watch historical films or read historical books. Even why they might be interested in history?
- Why were they popular? Class notes
- Who was Henry IV? Class notes. These give background and context to the play so that it makes sense.
- How to quote text. Inverted comma + quoted line + Line breaks / + inverted comma + play title + act = roman numerals + scene = numbers.
- Pack up.
Lesson reflection:

What is a history play?
A history play is the name given to the collection of Shakespeare's plays published by The Kings Men after his death, that relate to the Kings of England. The bulk of these plays make up two tetrologies of plays called The Henriead, meaning the plays Richard II, The Two parts of Henry IV and Henry V. And the second, The Margaretsaga, comprising of the three Henry VI plays and Richard III. The plays King John, Edward III and Henry VIII complete the collection of History plays. At the time of writing these plays would not however have been recognised as "histories". Richard II and Richard III are both published as tragedies during Shakespeare's life. While Henry IV parts 1 and 2 focus as much on the comic goings on of the old knight Sir Jack Falstaff as they do the political uprisings that beset The king.

Why were they popular?
These plays were incredibly popular amongst Elizabethan audiences, as were the Chronicles from which these plays were sourced. In the wake of attempted invasion by the Spanish, the population of London was eager for stories about England's greatness in the world. Shakespeare was not the only writer working in London to write history plays. History plays were a way for playwrights to comment on the past glories or misadventures of long dead monarchs, as well as providing an opportunity to comment on the current monarch. Shakespeare only stopped writing plays about the Kings of England's past due to "The Bishops' Ban" on plays drawn from English history, after Heyward's History of Henry IV was banned and burned for its support for the rebellious Earl of Essex and implied criticism of the Crown.

Who was Henry IV?
King of England from 30 September 1399 – 20 March 1413, Henry IV was a grandson to King Edward III and cousin to King Richard II. As cousin to the King, Henry was a close companion. buHowever, as a young man he participated in a rebellion against Richard, though was not punished. He spent much of his 20's crusading in Lithuania and Jerusalem, before returning to England. In 1398 he and another nobleman, Thomas Mowbray, quarrelled and in lieu of a duel both were exiled, Henry for seven years and Mowbray for life. In 1399, after his father's death and Richard's seizure of his inheritance, Henry returned from exile to challenge the King. Although Henry claimed to only want his inheritance back, he soon found himself with enough support to take the crown from his cousin.

Henry would reign until 1413. His reign would be characterised by his need to protect himself against, plots, rebellions and assassination attempts.

He was the father of Henry V who won significant victories over the French during his reign and was a beloved and admired king by subsequent generations.

Stage: 5 **Topic: Act I Scene 1 Henry IV Part 1** **Lesson: 2**

Learning Intention: To begin exploring Henry IV Part 1, understanding the characters and the orientation of the play.

Teaching strategy: explicit teaching AV material and class discussion towards the creation of notes.

Presentation:
- Settle class and Roll.
- Hand out play script of and watch Act I Scene 1 of Henry IV Part 1. Students keep and annotate handouts until they have the entire play.
- After watching brainstorm with the students:
- What has just happened?
- Who has been introduced? What do we know about them?
- What conflict has been introduced?
- Students write a short paragraph answering each of these questions after class discussions.
- Students write the beginnings of a character profile for the following characters:
- Henry IV
- Pack up

Lesson reflection:

Character profile

What they do - actions and reactions	
What they say - statements and responses.	
How they say it - register, modality,	
What 'friends' say about them - positive aspects	
What 'enemies' say about them - negative aspects	

Stage: 5 **Topic: Act I Scene 2 Henry IV Part 1** **Lesson: 3**

Learning Intention: To begin exploring Henry IV Part 1, understanding the characters and the orientation of the play.

Teaching strategy: explicit teaching AV material and class discussion towards the creation of notes.

Presentation:
- Settle class and Roll.
- Hand out play script of and watch Act I Scene 2 of Henry IV Part 1.
- After watching brainstorm with the students:
- What has just happened?
- Who has been introduced? What do we know about them?
- What conflict has been introduced?
- Students write a short paragraph answering each of these questions after class discussions.
- Students write the beginnings of a character profile for the following characters:
- Falstaff
- Prince Hal
- Poins
- Pack up

Lesson reflection:

Stage: 5 **Topic: Act I Scene 3 Henry IV Part 1** **Lesson: 4**

Learning Intention: To begin exploring Henry IV Part 1, understanding the characters and the orientation of the play.

Teaching strategy: explicit teaching AV material and class discussion towards the creation of notes.

Presentation:
- Settle class and Roll.
- Hand out play script of and watch Act I Scene 3 of Henry IV Part 1.
- After watching brainstorm with the students:
- What has just happened?
- Who has been introduced? What do we know about them?
- What conflict has been introduced?
- Students write a short paragraph answering each of these questions after class discussions.
- Students write the beginnings of a character profile and add to existing profile for the following characters:
- Henry IV
- Henry Percy (Hotspur)
- Henry Percy Earl of Northumberland
- Thomas Percy Earl of Worchester
- Pack up

Lesson reflection:

Stage: 5   **Topic:** Act I Henry IV Part 1 - Themes   **Lesson: 5**

Learning Intention: To begin exploring Henry IV Part 1, understanding the themes and the structure of the play.

Teaching strategy: explicit teaching and class discussion towards the creation of notes.

Presentation:

- Settle class and Roll.
- Plot lines – Students draw up a table in their books with these headings: Henry IV and Rebels, Hal and Falstaff, Hal and Henry IV. Under each heading put the major plot points that relate to each pairing. This will be a document that the students add to so make sure that they leave enough room for the five acts.
- Themes – What themes or main ideas are developing in this first act of the play? For each plot thread have students identify what the major theme of that narrative arc might be? Students can attach quotes to the theme to back up their predictions.
- Students write a short paragraph answering each of these questions after class discussions using their own words with details.
- Have students write a short narrative predicting where the play will go from here.
- Pack up

Lesson reflection:

Stage: 5   Topic: Act II Scenes 1 and 2 Henry IV Part 1   Lesson: 6

Learning Intention: To continue exploring Henry IV Part 1, understanding the characters, themes and structure of the play.

Teaching strategy: explicit teaching AV material and class discussion towards the creation of notes.

Presentation:
- Settle class and Roll.
- Hand out play script of and watch Act II Scenes 1 and 2
- After watching brainstorm with the students:
- What has just happened?
- What new characters have been introduced?
- Students write a short paragraph answering each of these questions after class discussions using their own words with details.
- Pack up

Lesson reflection:

Stage: 5 **Topic: Act II Scene 3 Henry IV Part 1** **Lesson: 7**

Learning Intention: To continue exploring Henry IV Part 1, understanding the characters, themes and structure of the play.

Teaching strategy: explicit teaching AV material and class discussion towards the creation of notes.

Presentation:
- Settle class and Roll.
- Hand out play script of and watch Act II Scene 3
- After watching brainstorm with the students:
- What has just happened?
- What new characters have been introduced?
- Compare and contrast Hal and Hotspur. Back up your claims about each with evidence from the play, using quotes and/or actions.
- Students write a short paragraph answering each of these questions after class discussions using their own words with details.
- Pack up

Lesson reflection:

Stage: 5   Topic: Act II Scene 4 Henry IV Part 1   Lesson: 8

Learning Intention: To continue exploring Henry IV Part 1, understanding the characters, themes and structure of the play.

Teaching strategy: explicit teaching AV material and class discussion towards the creation of notes.

Presentation:
- Settle class and Roll.
- Hand out play script of and watch Act II Scene 4
- After watching brainstorm with the students:
- What has just happened?
- This is the longest scene in the play. Why do you think it is so important? How does it relate to the themes?
- Students write a short paragraph answering each of these questions after class discussions using their own words with details.
- Pack up

Lesson reflection:

Stage: 5   **Topic:** Act II Scene 4 Henry IV Part 1   **Lesson:** 9

Learning Intention: To continue exploring Henry IV Part 1, understanding the characters, themes and structure of the play.

Teaching strategy: explicit teaching, AV material and class discussion towards the creation of notes.

Presentation:
- Settle class and Roll.
- Watch Act II Scene 4 up to the entry of Falstaff with the message from court.
- After watching brainstorm with the students:
- Hal jokes about honour, and commanding the good opinion of the drawers of Eastcheap, later he compares his state unfavourably with Hotspur. What does this tell us about Hal?
- Why is Falstaff angry?
- Why does he call Hal and Poins cowards?
- Why is this ironic and funny coming from Falstaff?
- How big does Falstaff's face saving story become?
- What is his reaction when Hal says he and Poins robbed them?
- In what way can we see Falstaff as Hal's father figure?
- Students write a short paragraph answering each of these questions after class discussions using their own words with details. Make sure to include quotes and or examples of action from the play to back up your answers.
- Pack up

Lesson reflection:

Stage: 5   **Topic: Act II Scene 4 Henry IV Part 1**   **Lesson: 10**

Learning Intention: To continue exploring Henry IV Part 1, understanding the characters, themes and structure of the play.

Teaching strategy: explicit teaching AV material and class discussion towards the creation of notes.

Presentation:
- Settle class and Roll.
- Watch Act II Scene 4 from the entry of Falstaff with the message from court to the end of the scene.
- After watching brainstorm with the students:
- What is the message Falstaff brings? How does it change the mood? How do Hal and Falstaff between them bring the mood back up?
- Hal also has to appear before his father at court tomorrow how does Falstaff suggest he proceed?
- How does Falstaff play the King? What do we see is Falstaff's motivation?
- Why does Hal insist they switch places? How does Hal bring the play to a conclusion?
- The sheriff's arrival sends everyone into a panic. How does Hal protect his friends and the robbery victims? Why is war a place for honour?
- How do we see Hal leaving this world behind as real danger encroaches?
- Students write a short paragraph answering each of these questions after class discussions using their own words with details. Make sure to include quotes and or examples of action from the play to back up your answers.
- Pack up

Lesson reflection:

Stage: 5   Topic: Act III Scene 1 Henry IV Part 1   Lesson: 11

Learning Intention: To continue exploring Henry IV Part 1, understanding the characters, themes and structure of the play.

Teaching strategy: explicit teaching AV material and class discussion towards the creation of notes.

Presentation:
- Settle class and Roll.
- Hand out play script of and watch Act III scene 1.
- After watching brainstorm with the students:
- What happens?
- Who is introduced?
- What seeds of disappointment are already being sewn amongst the rebels?
- Add to the narrative table using your own words with details.
- Students write a short paragraph answering each of these questions after class discussions using their own words with details. Make sure to include quotes and or examples of action from the play to back up your answers.
- Pack up

Lesson reflection:

Stage: 5   **Topic: Act III Scene 2 Henry IV Part**   **Lesson: 12**

Learning Intention: To continue exploring Henry IV Part 1, understanding the characters, themes and structure of the play.

Teaching strategy: explicit teaching AV material and class discussion towards the creation of notes.

Presentation:
- Settle class and Roll.
- Hand out play scripts and watch Act III Scene 2.
- After watching brainstorm with the students:
- What happens?
- How is Hal different in the presence of the King compared to how we have seen him so far?
- Compare and contrast Falstaff and Henry IV as father figures.
- Students write a short paragraph answering each of these questions after class discussions using their own words with details. Make sure to include quotes and or examples of action from the play to back up your answers.
- Add to the narrative table using your own words with details.
- Pack up

Lesson reflection:

Stage: 5 **Topic: Act III Scene 3 Henry IV Part 1** **Lesson: 13**

Learning Intention: To continue exploring Henry IV Part 1, understanding the characters, themes and structure of the play.

Teaching strategy: explicit teaching AV material and class discussion towards the creation of notes.

Presentation:
- Settle class and Roll.
- Hand out play scripts and watch Act III Scene 3
- After watching brainstorm with the students:
- What happens?
- How is Falstaff different away from Hal?
- How does Falstaff change when Hal enters?
- How is Hal different after his meeting with his father?
- Add to the narrative table using your own words with details.
- Students write a short paragraph answering each of these questions after class discussions using their own words with details. Make sure to include quotes and or examples of action from the play to back up your answers.
- Pack up

Lesson reflection:

Stage: 5   Topic: Act II and III Henry IV Part 1 - Themes   Lesson: 14

Learning Intention: To continue exploring Henry IV Part 1, understanding the themes and the structure of the play.

Teaching strategy: explicit teaching and class discussion towards the creation of notes.

Presentation:
- Settle class and Roll.
- Themes that have developed through this act are the ones that will dominate to remainder of the play.
- Was your theme prediction correct? Why? Why not?
- Find three examples in the text so far, either in quotes or actions of the characters and how they relate to the following themes.
- Honour and Dishonour. 3 examples for each.
- Strict Father (the King) and Indulgent Father (Falstaff). 3 examples for each.
- Pleasure and Duty. 3 examples for each.
- Students write a short paragraph answering each of these questions after class discussions using their own words with details.
- Pack up

Lesson reflection:

Stage: 5   Topic: Act II and III Henry IV Part 1 - Character   Lesson: 15

Learning Intention: To continue exploring Henry IV Part 1, understanding the characters of the play.

Teaching strategy: explicit teaching and class discussion towards the creation of notes.

Presentation:
- Settle class and Roll.
- Characters that have developed through this act are the ones that will dominate to remainder of the play.
- Have students add to their character charts for the following characters:
- Henry IV
- Hal
- Hotspur
- Falstaff
- Worcester
- Glendower
- Mortimer
- Pack up

Lesson reflection:

Stage: 5   **Topic: Act IV Scene 1 Henry IV Part 1**   **Lesson: 16**

Learning Intention: To continue exploring Henry IV Part 1, understanding the characters, themes and structure of the play.

Teaching strategy: explicit teaching AV material and class discussion towards the creation of notes.

Presentation:
- Settle class and Roll.
- Hand out play scripts and watch Act IV Scene 1
- After watching brainstorm with the students:
- What happens?
- What setback have the rebels suffered?
- How does Hotspur show his honour?
- Do Worcester, Vernon and Douglas share Hotspur's sentiments?
- Add to the narrative table using your own words with details.
- Students write a short paragraph answering each of these questions after class discussions using their own words with details. Make sure to include quotes and or examples of action from the play to back up your answers.
- Pack up

Lesson reflection:

Stage: 5   Topic: Act IV Scene 2 Henry IV Part 1   Lesson: 17

Learning Intention: To continue exploring Henry IV Part 1, understanding the characters, themes and structure of the play.

Teaching strategy: explicit teaching AV material and class discussion towards the creation of notes.

Presentation:
- Settle class and Roll.
- Hand out play scripts and watch Act IV Scene 2
- After watching brainstorm with the students:
- What happens?
- What has Falstaff done with the orders he has been given to bring men for the battle?
- This scene has been known as Pooh-Bear in armour. While technically a knight, how does Falstaff undermine everything a knight is supposed to stand for?
- Why do you think this scene comes straight after the one which shows Hotspur as such ah honourable warrior?
- What does this scene show us about Falstaff's esteem in the eyes of Hal?
- Add to the narrative table using your own words with details.
- Students write a short paragraph answering each of these questions after class discussions using their own words with details. Make sure to include quotes and or examples of action from the play to back up your answers.
- Pack up

Lesson reflection:

Stage: 5   Topic: Act IV Scene 3 and 4 Henry IV Part 1   Lesson: 18

Learning Intention: To continue exploring Henry IV Part 1, understanding the characters, themes and structure of the play.

Teaching strategy: explicit teaching AV material and class discussion towards the creation of notes.

Presentation:
- Settle class and Roll.
- Hand out play scripts and watch Act IV Scene 3 and 4
- After watching brainstorm with the students:
- What happens?
- Hotspur has a long speech in which he relates the injuries of honour his family has suffered at the hands of the King to Blunt. Does Blunt seem impressed?
- Why do you think Hotspur doesn't even send this message to the king in the end?
- Scene 4 What happens?
- Why is there a scene with the Archbishop? A clue is in the title of the play.
- Does this scene add anything?
- Why introduce new characters at this point?
- Add to the narrative table using your own words with details.
- Students write a short paragraph answering each of these questions after class discussions using their own words with details. Make sure to include quotes and or examples of action from the play to back up your answers.
-Pack up

Lesson reflection:

Stage: 5   **Topic: Act IV Henry IV Part 1 - Themes**   **Lesson: 19**

Learning Intention: To continue exploring Henry IV Part 1, understanding the themes and the structure of the play.

Teaching strategy: explicit teaching and class discussion towards the creation of notes.

Presentation:
- Settle class and Roll.
- What themes have come to the fore in this act?
- Why are we now focusing on honour so much?
- How is honour expressed in this act?
- How do we see less scrupulous people use Hotspur's blunt and honourable nature against him? Is Hotspur as politically astute as his uncle Worchester, the Archbishop, King Henry or even Hal?
- Students write a short paragraph answering each of these questions after class discussions using their own words with details. Students can work in pairs.
- Students report back their answers as a class discussion.
- Pack up

Lesson reflection:

Stage: 5   Topic: Act IV Henry IV Part 1 - Character   Lesson: 20

Learning Intention: To continue exploring Henry IV Part 1, understanding the themes and the structure of the play.

Teaching strategy: explicit teaching and class discussion towards the creation of notes.

Presentation:
- Settle class and Roll.
- Add to your character charts for the following characters
- Hal
- Hotspur
- Falstaff
- Worcester
- Vernon
- Choose one of these characters on the eve of battle and write a diary entry about why they are here, what they hope the next day will bring, and their fears. Write in the present tense and try to use the kind of language that the character uses in the play.
- Pack up

Lesson reflection:

Stage: 5   **Topic: Act V Scene 1 Henry IV Part 1**   **Lesson: 21**

Learning Intention: To continue exploring Henry IV Part 1, understanding the characters, themes and structure of the play.

Teaching strategy: explicit teaching AV material and class discussion towards the creation of notes.

Presentation:
- Settle class and Roll.
- Hand out play scripts and watch Act V Scene 1
- After watching brainstorm with the students:
- What happens?
- Worcester now has a long speech in which he relates the injuries of honour his family has suffered at the hands of the King. How does the king respond?
- How is Hal different in this scene than we have seen him before?
- Why does Hal offer to fight Hotspur in single combat?
- What do you think of Falstaff's catechism on honour at the end of this scene? Why do you think Shakespeare chooses to undercut the chivalric tone of the scene with this speech at the end?
- Add to the narrative table using your own words with details.
- Students write a short paragraph answering each of these questions after class discussions using their own words with details. Make sure to include quotes and or examples of action from the play to back up your answers.
- Pack up

Lesson reflection:

Stage: 5   Topic: Act V Scene 2 and 3 Henry IV Part 1   Lesson: 22

Learning Intention: To continue exploring Henry IV Part 1, understanding the characters, themes and structure of the play.

Teaching strategy: explicit teaching AV material and class discussion towards the creation of notes.

Presentation:
- Settle class and Roll.
- Hand out play scripts and watch Act V Scene 2 and 3
- After watching brainstorm with the students:
- What happens?
- Why do Worcester and Vernon not tell Hotspur about the King's offer?
- What does this tell us about their understanding of honour? How can they be seen to be using Hotspur?
- Why is Vernon again impressed by Hal? How does Hotspur regard Hal?

Scene 3
- How do we see honour played out in this scene? Give examples for the following characters:
- Blunt
- King Henry
- Falstaff
- Hal
- Add to the narrative table using your own words with details.
- Students write a short paragraph answering each of these questions after class discussions using their own words with details. Make sure to include quotes and or examples of action from the play to back up your answers.
- Pack up

Lesson reflection:

Stage: 5   **Topic:** Act V Scene 4 Henry IV Part 1   **Lesson:** 23

Learning Intention: To continue exploring Henry IV Part 1, understanding the characters, themes and structure of the play.

Teaching strategy: explicit teaching AV material and class discussion towards the creation of notes.

Presentation:
- Settle class and Roll.
- Hand out play scripts and watch Act V Scene 4
- After watching brainstorm with the students:
- What happens?
- Why does the king want Hal to leave the battle? Why does he refuse?
- How does Hal show that he is worthy of his title Prince of Wales?
- When does he claim his name and title?
- Hal and Hotspur never meet before this fight why do you think they are kept apart until this moment?
- Why is Falstaff in this scene?
- How does Falstaff again undercut the chivalric ideas of honour and valour in the scene?
- What do you think Shakespeare is trying to say about war?
- Add to the narrative table using your own words with details.
- Students write a short paragraph answering each of these questions after class discussions using their own words with details. Make sure to include quotes and or examples of action from the play to back up your answers.
- Pack up

Lesson reflection:

Stage: 5   **Topic: Act V Scene 5 Henry IV Part 1**   **Lesson: 24**

Learning Intention: To continue exploring Henry IV Part 1, understanding the characters, themes and structure of the play.

Teaching strategy: explicit teaching AV material and class discussion towards the creation of notes.

Presentation:

- Settle class and Roll.
- Hand out play scripts and watch Act V Scene 5
- After watching brainstorm with the students:
- What happens?
- Why are Worcester and Vernon to be executed?
- What is the fate of Lord Douglas?
- Has this battle finally achieved peace?
- How has Hal changed from the young man we met at the beginning of the play?
- What are your overall impressions of the play? Did the ending match up to your predictions at the beginning of the play?
- Add to the narrative table using your own words with details.
- Students write a short paragraph answering each of these questions after class discussions using their own words with details. Make sure to include quotes and or examples of action from the play to back up your answers.
- Pack up

Lesson reflection:

Stage: 5   **Topic: Act V Henry IV Part 1 - Themes**   **Lesson: 25**

Learning Intention: To continue exploring Henry IV Part 1, understanding the themes and the structure of the play.

Teaching strategy: explicit teaching and class discussion towards the creation of notes.

Presentation:
- Settle class and Roll.
- Was your theme prediction correct? Why? Why not?
- Find three examples in the text so far, either in quotes or actions of the characters and how they relate to the following themes.
- Honour and Dishonour. 3 examples for each.
- Strict Father (the King) and Indulgent Father (Falstaff). 3 examples for each.
- Pleasure and Duty. 3 examples for each.
- Family Loyalty and Loyalty to the King. 3 examples for each.
- Students write a short paragraph answering each of these questions after class discussions using their own words with details. Students can work together in pairs
- Students report back their answers as a class discussion.
- Pack up

Lesson reflection:

Julius Caesar

Year 10 Unit.

Stage: 5 **Topic: Introduce Julius Caesar** **Lesson: 1**

Learning Intention: To introduce the genre of tragedy as Shakespeare understood it and background to the play Julius Caesar.

Teaching strategy: Explicit teaching and class notes
Presentation:
- Settle class and Roll.
- What is tragedy?
- Talk to the class about why we like to watch dark stories?
- Who was Julius Caesar? Class notes. These give background and context to the play so that it makes sense.
- How to quote text. Inverted comma + quoted line + Line breaks / + inverted comma + play title + act = roman numerals + scene = numbers.
- Pack up

Lesson reflection:

What is Tragedy?

Tragedy is an ancient genre of play, dating back the to Ancient Greeks. The Tragedies all follow the idea that a fatal flaw or grievous error causes the downfall and suffering of the tragic hero. The exception to this model is the revenge tragedy, which was popular from the 1580's, this type of tragedy involves a wrong being committed against the tragic hero, who must avenge the wrong even at the cost of their own lives. Other tragedies are created through misunderstanding or manipulation. The moment blood is shed in a tragedy it can only end one way. Despite its often gloomy subject matter, and the fact that a great many deaths are involved in these plays, Tragedy was and is an extremely popular form of theatre. This is because of the action of catharsis. Tragedy provides a safe socially acceptable outlet for extreme and negative emotions. Because of the propensity of Elizabethan audiences to wander away once their favourite actor had left the stage, the deaths in Shakespearean tragedies are always placed at the very end of the play. Because of this it is possible that Shakespeare played Julius Caesar, as he appears to have written parts for himself that were old men, he was balding. And or who disappear or are killed partway through the play.

Who was Julius Caesar?

Julius Caesar was a general and statesman in the late Republican period of Rome. A member of the Roman nobility, Caesar was a senator, Governor of a Roman province in Spain, Governor of Gaul and Consul and later Dictator of Rome. He used his military position to campaign and expand the Roman presence in Gaul while Governor and began the first of three Civil wars when he refused to disband his army on orders from the Senate upon his return to Rome. Caesar then fought a Civil war with Pompey, his old ally and head of the Republican forces. Defeating Pompey in Egypt, Caesar declared himself Dictator for life. Dictator was a position in the Roman political system, but it was usually a temporary position given in times of crisis. This act alienated Republican senators, who conspired to assassinate Julius Caesar in the senate house on the 15th of March 44BCE.

Character profile

What they do - actions and reactions	
What they say - statements and responses.	
How they say it - register, modality,	
What 'friends' say about them - positive aspects	
What 'enemies' say about them - negative aspects	

Stage: 5   Topic: Act I Scene 1 Julius Caesar   Lesson: 2

Learning Intention: To begin exploring Julius Caesar, understanding the characters and the orientation of the play.

Teaching strategy: explicit teaching AV material and class discussion towards the creation of notes.

Presentation:
- Settle class and Roll.
- Hand out play script of and watch Act I Scene 1 of Julius Caesar. Students keep and annotate handouts until they have the entire play.
- After watching brainstorm with the students:
- What has just happened?
- Who has been introduced? What do we know about them?
- What conflict has been introduced?
- We will not see any of these characters again. Why would the play start with the "mob" rather than the main characters?
- Students write a short paragraph answering each of these questions after class discussions using their own words with details.
- Pack up

Lesson reflection:

Stage: 5 **Topic: Act I Scene 2 Julius Caesar** **Lesson: 3**

Learning Intention: To begin exploring Julius Caesar, understanding the characters and the orientation of the play.

Teaching strategy: explicit teaching AV material and class discussion towards the creation of notes.

Presentation:

- Settle class and Roll.
- Hand out play script of and watch Act I Scene 2 of Julius Caesar.
- After watching brainstorm with the students:
- What has just happened?
- Who has been introduced? What do we know about them?
- What conflict has been introduced?
- Students write a short paragraph answering each of these questions after class discussions using their own words with details.
- Students write the beginnings of a character profile for the following characters:
- Brutus
- Cassius
- Caesar
- Antony
- Casca
- Pack up

Lesson reflection:

Stage: 5   **Topic: Act I Scene 3 Julius Caesar**   **Lesson: 4**

Learning Intention: To begin exploring Julius Caesar, understanding the characters and the orientation of the play.

Teaching strategy: explicit teaching AV material and class discussion towards the creation of notes.

Presentation:
- Settle class and Roll.
- Hand out play script of and watch Act I Scene 3 of Julius Caesar.
- After watching brainstorm with the students:
- What has just happened?
- Who has been introduced? What do we know about them?
- What conflict has been introduced?
- Students write a short paragraph answering each of these questions after class discussions using their own words with details.
- Students write the beginnings or further details of a character profile for the following characters:
- Cassius
- Casca
- Cicero
- Pack up

Lesson reflection:

Stage: 5 **Topic: Act I Julius Caesar - Themes** **Lesson: 5**

Learning Intention: To begin exploring Julius Caesar, understanding the themes and the structure of the play.

Teaching strategy: explicit teaching and class discussion towards the creation of notes.

Presentation:
- Settle class and Roll.
- At the opening of this play the audience is introduced to a lot of characters. Who is the main character? Why?
- If Julius Caesar is not the main character, what does he symbolise? Why does that make him a threat to the other characters. What other symbols do we see in the first act of the play?
Brainstorm these questions with the students as a class.
- Create a spider map with Caesar at the centre with Brutus, Cassius, Casca, and Cinna around him with their reasons to oppose him. Use quotes
- Have students write a short narrative predicting where the play will go from here.
- Pack up

Lesson reflection:

Stage: 5   Topic: Act II Scene 1 Julius Caesar   Lesson: 6

Learning Intention: To continue exploring Julius Caesar, understanding the characters, themes and structure of the play.

Teaching strategy: explicit teaching AV material and class discussion towards the creation of notes.

Presentation:
- Settle class and Roll.
- Hand out play script of and watch Act II Scene 1 up to Lucius announcing Cassius at the door.
- After watching brainstorm with the students:
- What has just happened?
- How is Brutus trying to persuade himself of the 'rightness' of Cassius' plan to assassinate Caesar?
- What arguments does Brutus put forward? How are they different from Cassius' arguments in Act 1?
- Has Caesar actually done any of the things Brutus plans to kill him for?
- Students write a short paragraph answering each of these questions after class discussions using their own words with details.
- Add to you character profile of Brutus.
- Pack up

Lesson reflection:

Stage: 5   **Topic: Act II Scene 1 Julius Caesar**   **Lesson: 7**

Learning Intention: To continue exploring Julius Caesar, understanding the characters, themes and structure of the play.

Teaching strategy: explicit teaching AV material and class discussion towards the creation of notes.

Presentation:

- Settle class and Roll.
- Hand out play script of and watch Act II Scene 1 from the entry of Cassius and the conspirators to their exit.
- After watching brainstorm with the students:
- What has just happened?
- In this scene we see Brutus as an idealist, and Cassius as a pragmatist.
- Define Idealist and Pragmatist.
- Cassius has a practical plan and enough supporters to assassinate Caesar, why does he need Brutus' support? How does Brutus' idealism make him seem to take the lead here?
- Brutus uses a lot of religious and medical language, "Sacrificers", "a dish fit for the gods", "Purgers" (something to make you throw up poison). How does this language persuade the others, that stabbing to death an unarmed man is a good thing?
- What dangers does Brutus' idealism make him overlook?
- Students write a short paragraph answering each of these questions after class discussions using their own words with details.
- Add to your spider map for Brutus and Cassius.
- Pack up

Lesson reflection:

Stage: 5   **Topic: Act II Scene 1 Julius Caesar**   **Lesson: 8**

Learning Intention: To continue exploring Julius Caesar, understanding the characters, themes and structure of the play.

Teaching strategy: explicit teaching AV material and class discussion towards the creation of notes.

Presentation:
- Settle class and Roll.
- Hand out play script of and watch Act II Scene 1 from entry of Portia to the end of the scene.
- After watching brainstorm with the students:
- What has just happened?
- This is a play about politics and war, why do we have this dialogue with Portia, who is part of Brutus' domestic world here? Why is he willing to bring her into the world of politics and tell her their plan?
- Again in this scene we see Caesar being discussed as an illness in Rome which must be cured. These men are plotting a murder, how does the language they use make it seem less real?
- Students write a short paragraph answering each of these questions after class discussions using their own words with details.
- Add to Brutus' character profile.
- Pack up

Lesson reflection:

Stage: 5 **Topic: Act II Scene 2 Julius Caesar** **Lesson: 9**

Learning Intention: To continue exploring Julius Caesar, understanding the characters, themes and structure of the play.

Teaching strategy: explicit teaching AV material and class discussion towards the creation of notes.

Presentation:
- Settle class and Roll.
- Hand out play script of and watch Act II Scene 2.
- After watching brainstorm with the students:
- What has just happened?
- Why does Calphurnia not want Caesar to go to the capital?
- Caesar shows himself to be both a private and a public figure in this scene. How does Calphurnia persuade the private human, Caesar to stay home?
- How does Descius Brutus persuade the 'public' Caesar to go to the capitol and ignore the fears of the private man?
- It would be easier for the conspirators to kill Caesar at home, as they are clearly welcome into his home. Why do they insist on bringing him to the Senate house to be killed? Who are they trying to kill, the private man or the public figure?
- Students write a short paragraph answering each of these questions after class discussions using their own words with details.
- Pack up

Lesson reflection:

Stage: 5   Topic: Act II Scenes 3 and 4 Julius Caesar   Lesson: 10

Learning Intention: To continue exploring Julius Caesar, understanding the characters, themes and structure of the play.

Teaching strategy: explicit teaching AV material and class discussion towards the creation of notes.

Presentation:
- Settle class and Roll.
- Hand out play script of and watch Act II Scenes 3 and 4.
- After watching brainstorm with the students:
- What has just happened?
- Why are these scenes here? What do they add?
- This is the last time we see women in this play. How does Portia represent the apprehension of the conspirators?
- In a play filled with soothsayers, dreams and other superstitious visions, all symbolising a sick Rome, are we the audience being manipulated into believing that the illness is Caesar? Are we the audience too easily persuaded that the conspiracy is correct? Is this a chance to pause and reflect before the point of no return?
- Students write a short paragraph answering each of these questions after class discussions using their own words with details.
- Pack up

Lesson reflection:

Stage: 5 **Topic: Act II Julius Caesar - Themes** **Lesson: 11**

Learning Intention: To continue exploring Julius Caesar, understanding the themes and the structure of the play.

Teaching strategy: explicit teaching and class discussion towards the creation of notes.

Presentation:
- Settle class and Roll.
- Themes that have developed through this act are the ones that will dominate to remainder of the play.
- Was your theme prediction correct? Why? Why not?
- Find three examples in the text so far, either in quotes or actions of the characters and how they relate to the following themes.
- Idealism and Self interest. 3 examples for each.
- Persuasion and manipulation. 3 examples for each.
- Legitimate rule and tyranny. 3 examples for each.
- Public and private figures. 3 examples for each.
- Students write a short paragraph answering each of these questions after class discussions using their own words with details.
- Students share their individual responses in a class discussion.
- Pack up

Lesson reflection:

Stage: 5   **Topic: Act III Scene 1 Julius Caesar**   **Lesson: 12**

Learning Intention: To continue exploring Julius Caesar, understanding the characters, themes and structure of the play.

Teaching strategy: explicit teaching AV material and class discussion towards the creation of notes.

Presentation:
- Settle class and Roll.
- Hand out play script of and watch Act III Scene 1.
- After watching brainstorm with the students:
- What has just happened?
- How does Brutus try to control the situation after the assassination and ritualise it?
- Why is Marc Antony a problem and how does Brutus try to neutralise it?
- Is Marc Antony the careless, party animal the conspirators portray him as? How is he far more than their estimation?
- Students write a short paragraph answering each of these questions after class discussions using their own words with details.
Add to your character profiles for Brutus, Cassius and Marc Antony.
- Pack up

Lesson reflection:

Stage: 5 **Topic: Act III Scene 2 Julius Caesar** **Lesson: 13**

Learning Intention: To continue exploring Julius Caesar, understanding the characters, themes and structure of the play.

Teaching strategy: explicit teaching AV material and class discussion towards the creation of notes.

Presentation:
- Settle class and Roll.
- Hand out play script of and watch Act III Scene 2.
- After watching brainstorm with the students:
- What has just happened?
- How does Brutus try persuade the mob? Brutus usually speaks in verse, why when talking to the common folk does he talk in prose? What does this tell us about Brutus?
- Why does Marc Antony choose to manipulate the mob's emotions? He doesn't speak to them as equals as Brutus did. Antony speaks in verse, but connects with the Mob far better then Brutus. What does this tell us about how Antony sees the crowd?
- Why does emotion work better than reason to inflame the crowd?
- Why does Antony want to inspire the mob to riot?
- Students write a short paragraph answering each of these questions after class discussions using their own words with details.

Add to your character profile for Brutus and Marc Antony.
- Pack up

Lesson reflection:

Stage: 5   Topic: Act III Scene 3 and Act IV Scene 1 Julius Caesar
Lesson: 14

Learning Intention: To continue exploring Julius Caesar, understanding the characters, themes and structure of the play.

Teaching strategy: explicit teaching AV material and class discussion towards the creation of notes.

Presentation:
- Settle class and Roll.
- Hand out play script of and watch Act III Scene 3 and Act IV Scene 1.
- After watching brainstorm with the students:
    - What has just happened?
    - Antony's speech has inspired a riot. How can we see that this was his goal all along? Look back at the end of Act III Scene 2.
    - Antony, Octavius and Lepidus are very coldly marking out rivals and enemies for death. Have the conspirators made their world any freer, by their actions, or more tyrannical?
    - The power dynamics between the three are unbalanced, who is the weakest member of this trio?
- Students write a short paragraph answering each of these questions after class discussions using their own words with details.
Add to your character profile for Marc Antony.
- Pack up
Lesson reflection:

Stage: 5   **Topic: Act III Julius Caesar - Themes**   **Lesson: 15**

Learning Intention: To continue exploring Julius Caesar, understanding the themes and the structure of the play.

Teaching strategy: explicit teaching and class discussion towards the creation of notes.

Presentation:

- Settle class and Roll.
- Love is a word mentioned frequently in all acts of the play, create a mind map of love and how the different loves expressed by the characters brings them into conflict.
- Find three examples in the text so far, either in quotes or actions of the characters and how they relate to the following themes.
- Idea and Action. 3 examples for each.
- Intellect and Emotion. 3 examples for each.
- Chaos and Order. 3 examples for each.
- Students write a short paragraph answering each of these questions after class discussions using their own words with details.
- Students share their individual responses in a class discussion.
- Pack up

Lesson reflection:

Stage: 5   **Topic: Act II Julius Caesar - Characters**   **Lesson: 16**

Learning Intention: To continue exploring Julius Caesar, understanding the characters and their motivations within the play.

Teaching strategy: explicit teaching and class discussion towards the creation of notes.

Presentation:
- Settle class and Roll.
- Marc Antony has been spoken about and seen briefly, what do we learn about him in this act?
- Is he more or less of a threat than the conspirator's feared?
- Is Marc Antony more or less of a threat than Caesar was? If Caesar may have made himself king, what is Marc Antony threatening to become?
- What do you think happens next?
- Students write a short paragraph answering each of these questions after class discussions using their own words with details.
- Pack up

Lesson reflection:

Stage: 5   Topic: Act IV Scenes 2 and 3 Julius Caesar   Lesson: 17

Learning Intention: To continue exploring Julius Caesar, understanding the characters, themes and structure of the play.

Teaching strategy: explicit teaching AV material and class discussion towards the creation of notes.

Presentation:
- Settle class and Roll.
- Hand out play script of and watch Act IV Scenes 2 and 3 up to the entry of Tittinius and Messala.
- After watching brainstorm with the students:
- What has just happened?
- How is Brutus and Cassius' relationship?
- Why do Brutus and Cassius argue?
- How is this affecting Brutus particularly? What has happened to Portia?
- Students write a short paragraph answering each of these questions after class discussions using their own words with details.

Add to your character profiles for Brutus and Cassius.

- Pack up

Lesson reflection:

Stage: 5   Topic: Act IV Scene 3 Julius Caesar   Lesson: 18

Learning Intention: To continue exploring Julius Caesar, understanding the characters, themes and structure of the play.

Teaching strategy: explicit teaching AV material and class discussion towards the creation of notes.

Presentation:
- Settle class and Roll.
- Hand out play script of and watch Act IV Scene 3 from the entry of Tittinius and Messala.
- After watching brainstorm with the students:
- What has just happened?
- What have Antony, Octavian and Lepidus been doing to the conspirators and their supporters in Rome?
- How is Brutus' reaction to news about Portia different when he is no longer alone? What does this say about how he like Caesar is both a public and a private man?
- Why does Cassius, a more seasoned general, defer to Brutus in choosing to meet Antony's forces a Philippi?
- Why can't Brutus sleep alone? What does he see?
- Students write a short paragraph answering each of these questions after class discussions using their own words with details.

Add to your character profiles for Brutus and Cassius.
- Pack up

Lesson reflection:

Stage: 5   Topic: Act IV Julius Caesar - Themes   Lesson: 19

Learning Intention: To continue exploring Julius Caesar, understanding the themes and the structure of the play.

Teaching strategy: explicit teaching and class discussion towards the creation of notes.

Presentation:
- Settle class and Roll.
- Has killing Caesar produced the results that the conspirators were expecting?
- Brutus likes order, how can we see the world becoming more disordered in the wake of Caesar's death?
- Find three examples in the text so far, either in quotes or actions of the characters and how they relate to the following themes.
- Idealism and Self interest. 3 examples for each.
- Chaos and Order. 3 examples for each.
- Rule of law and Rule by fear. 3 examples for each.
- Public and private figures. 3 examples for each.
- Students write a short paragraph answering each of these questions after class discussions using their own words with details.
- Students share their individual responses in a class discussion.
- Pack up

Lesson reflection:

Stage: 5   Topic: Act IV Julius Caesar - Characters   Lesson: 20

Learning Intention: To continue exploring Julius Caesar, understanding the characters and their motivations within the play.

Teaching strategy: explicit teaching and class discussion towards the creation of notes.

Presentation:
- Settle class and Roll.
- What can we tell about the relationship between Brutus and Cassius from this act?
- Is it equal?
- Has it ever been equal?
- What do you think happens next?
- Students write a short paragraph answering each of these questions after class discussions using their own words with details. Students can work in pairs.
- Students share their individual responses in a class discussion.
- Pack up

Lesson reflection:

Stage: 5 **Topic: Act V Scene 1 Julius Caesar** **Lesson: 21**

Learning Intention: To continue exploring Julius Caesar, understanding the characters, themes and structure of the play.

Teaching strategy: explicit teaching AV material and class discussion towards the creation of notes.

Presentation:
- Settle class and Roll.
- Hand out play script of and watch Act V Scene 1.
- After watching brainstorm with the students:
- What has just happened?
- How is Antony and Octavius' relationship?
- Are Brutus and Cassius as confidant of victory as they make out?
- Students write a short paragraph answering each of these questions after class discussions using their own words with details.

Add to your character profiles for, Antony, Octavian, Brutus and Cassius.

- Pack up

Lesson reflection:

Stage: 5   Topic: Act V Scenes 2 and 3 Julius Caesar   Lesson: 22

Learning Intention: To continue exploring Julius Caesar, understanding the characters, themes and structure of the play.

Teaching strategy: explicit teaching AV material and class discussion towards the creation of notes.

Presentation:
- Settle class and Roll.
- Hand out play script of and watch Act V Scenes 2 and 3.
- After watching brainstorm with the students:
- What has just happened?
- How does misunderstanding and miscommunication caused Cassius' death?
- How does misunderstanding and miscommunication lose the battle?
- What does Brutus mean when he says "O Julius Caesar, thou art mighty yet!"?
- Students write a short paragraph answering each of these questions after class discussions using their own words with details.

Add to your character profiles for Brutus and Cassius.
- Pack up

Lesson reflection:

Stage: 5 Topic: Act V Scenes 4 and 5 Julius Caesar Lesson: 23

Learning Intention: To continue exploring Julius Caesar, understanding the characters, themes and structure of the play.

Teaching strategy: explicit teaching AV material and class discussion towards the creation of notes.

Presentation:

- Settle class and Roll.
- Hand out play script of and watch Act V Scenes 4 and 5.
- After watching brainstorm with the students:
- What has just happened?
- Why does Lucilius say he is Brutus?
- Why does Brutus choose to die rather than be captured?
- Octavius takes the last words from Antony, why do you think this is?
- Students write a short paragraph answering each of these questions after class discussions using their own words with details.

Add to your character profiles for Antony, Octavius and Brutus.

- Pack up

Lesson reflection:

Stage: 5   **Topic: Act V Julius Caesar - Themes**   **Lesson: 24**

Learning Intention: To continue exploring Julius Caesar, understanding the themes and the structure of the play.

Teaching strategy: explicit teaching and class discussion towards the creation of notes.

Presentation:
- Settle class and Roll.
- Octavian is called Caesar in this act. How can we see the public Caesar is more difficult to kill than the private man was? How is this ideal of Caesar more dangerous than the living man ever was?
- Find three examples in the text so far, either in quotes or actions of the characters and how they relate to the following themes.
- Idealism and Self interest. 3 examples for each.
- Love and Rivalry. 3 examples for each.
- Public and private figures. 3 examples for each.
- Students write a short paragraph answering each of these questions after class discussions using their own words with details. Students can work in pairs.
- Students share their individual responses in a class discussion.
- Pack up

Lesson reflection:

Stage: 5   Topic: Act V Julius Caesar - Characters   Lesson: 25

Learning Intention: To continue exploring Julius Caesar, understanding the characters and their motivations within the play.

Teaching strategy: explicit teaching and class discussion towards the creation of notes.

Presentation:
- Settle class and Roll.
- Who is the hero of this play?
- What makes him tragic?
- Why then is it called Julius Caesar? What does he represent?
- Students write a short paragraph answering each of these questions after class discussions using their own words with details. Students can work in pairs.
- Students share their individual responses in a class discussion.
- Pack up

Lesson reflection:

The Taming of the Shrew

Year 10 Unit.

Stage: 5   **Topic: Introducing Taming of the Shrew**   **Lesson: 1**

Learning Intention: Introduce The Taming of the Shrew and watch the prologue.

Teaching strategy: Direct instruction and AV media
Presentation:
- Settle class and Roll.
- What is the play about?
- Talk with the children about why they watch comedy films or read comedy books.
- Does knowing something is a comedy change the way that an audience "reads" it?
- Comedy in Elizabethan England? - Class notes. These give background and context to the play so that it makes sense.
- How to quote text. Inverted comma + quoted line + Line breaks / + inverted comma + play title + act = roman numerals + scene = numbers.
- Pack up

Lesson reflection:

Elizabethan Comedy.
Some quarters of polite and educated Elizabethan Society held a great suspicion of comedy and of theatre in general. These critics saw comedy as a disruptive force, while supporters saw the educational possibilities of comic theatre. Because the focus of the comedies is the restoration of order that has some how been disrupted at the outset or during the beginning of the play, this was seen as a general good. The idea that a comedy held a mirror up to the world and reflected it back to the audience, meant that some people criticised comedies for being frivollous and encouraging misbehaviour in the audience. While supporters defended it as showing how a properly intergrated society should work after the chaos of the plot. The Comedies are the plays that generally focus on courtship and usually end with marriage. Their drama is often predicated upon misunderstanding and confusion, that can be easily untangled. The stakes can be quite high, but the resolution is always peaceful and non-violent. Some of the Comedies can be quite dark, but they are always resolved without bloodshed.

What is The Taming of the Shrew?
The Taming of the Shrew is a comedy by Shakespeare. It is a comedy from very early in his career and we don't actually know much about who it was composed for or what sources he used to write the story. We do know that stories about Shrewish women and their meaner cousins Viragoes were very popular during the early 1590's when this play is thought to have been composed. It tells the story of the wooing of Katherine a gentlewoman, of vile disposition from Padua by Petruchio. Contrasted by the courtship of her sister Bianca, a very proper girl, and her many suitors. The play is also a play within a play, put on for the entertainment of a drunken man Christopher Sly who has been dressed up as a nobleman for the entertainment of the local nobleman. As plays go this is one of the most curiously constructed ones in the whole of Shakespeare's works.

Stage: 5	Topic: Prologue Taming of the Shrew	Lesson: 2

Learning Intention: Introduce The Taming of the Shrew and watch the prologue.

Teaching strategy: Direct instruction and AV media
Presentation:
- Settle class and Roll.
- Hand out play script of and watch the Prologue. Students keep and annotate handouts until they have the entire play.
- Class discusses first impressions of the prologue.
- What is happening?
- What conflict is in the prologue?
- We won't see any of these characters again. Why start with them?
- Pack up

Lesson reflection:

Stage: 5   Topic: Act I Scene 1 The Taming of the Shrew   Lesson: 3

Learning Intention: To begin exploring The Taming of the Shrew, understanding the characters and the orientation of the play.

Teaching strategy: explicit teaching AV material and class discussion towards the creation of notes.

Presentation:
- Settle class and Roll.
- Hand out play script of and watch Act I Scene 1 of The Taming of the Shrew.
- After watching brainstorm with the students:
- What has just happened?
- Who has been introduced? What do we know about them?
- What conflict has been introduced?
- How does this relate to the prologue?
- Students write a short paragraph answering each of these questions after class discussions. Students should reword each question to start their answers.
- Students write the beginnings of a character profile for the following characters:
- Lucentio
- Tranio
- Hortensio
- Gremio
- Katherina
- Bianca
- Baptista
- Pack up

Lesson reflection:

Character profile

What they do - actions and reactions	
What they say - statements and responses.	
How they say it - register, modality,	
What 'friends' say about them - positive aspects	
What 'enemies' say about them - negative aspects	

Stage: 5   Topic: Act I Scene 2 The Taming of the Shrew   Lesson: 4

Learning Intention: To begin exploring The Taming of the Shrew, understanding the characters and the orientation of the play.

Teaching strategy: explicit teaching AV material and class discussion towards the creation of notes.

Presentation:
- Settle class and Roll.
- Hand out play script of and watch Act I Scene 2 of The Taming of the Shrew.
- After watching brainstorm with the students:
- What has just happened?
- Who has been introduced? What do we know about them?
- What conflict has been introduced?
- Students write a short paragraph answering each of these questions after class discussions.
- Students continue or begin character profiles for the following characters:
- Lucentio
- Tranio
- Hortensio
- Gremio
- Katherina
- Bianca
- Baptista
- Petruchio
- Pack up

Lesson reflection:

Stage: 5   Topic: Act I The Taming of the Shrew - Themes   Lesson: 5

Learning Intention: To begin exploring The Taming of the Shrew understanding the themes and the structure of the play.

Teaching strategy: explicit teaching and class discussion towards the creation of notes.

Presentation:

- Settle class and Roll.
- Plot lines – Students draw up a table in their books with these headings: Bianca & Suitors, Katherina and Petruchio, Lucentio and Tranio. Under each heading put the major plot points that relate to each pairing. This will be a document that the students add to so make sure that they leave enough room for the five acts.
- Themes – Disguise and authenticity is the major theme of this play. For each plot thread have students identify how this theme is playing out? Students can attach quotes to the theme to back up their predictions. Using the method to quote taught in lesson 1.
- Have students write a short narrative predicting where the play will go from here.
- Pack up

Lesson reflection:

Stage: 5   Topic: Act II Scene 1 The Taming of the Shrew   Lesson: 6

Learning Intention: To begin exploring The Taming of the Shrew, understanding the characters, themes and structure of the play.

Teaching strategy: explicit teaching AV material and class discussion towards the creation of notes.

Presentation:
- Settle class and Roll.
- Hand out play script of and watch Act II Scene 1 of The Taming of the Shrew.
- After watching brainstorm with the students:
- What has just happened?
- What disguises are being employed and by whom?
- Students write a short paragraph answering each of these questions after class discussions.
- Students write additions to the character profiles for the following characters:
- Lucentio
- Tranio
- Hortensio
- Gremio
- Bianca
- Baptista
- Pack up

Lesson reflection:

Stage: 5   Topic: Act II Scene 1 The Taming of the Shrew   Lesson: 7

Learning Intention: To begin exploring The Taming of the Shrew, understanding the characters, themes and structure of the play.

Teaching strategy: explicit teaching AV material and class discussion towards the creation of notes.

Presentation:
- Settle class and Roll.
- Hand out play script of and watch Act II Scene 1 of The Taming of the Shrew. Katherina Bianca and Baptista dialogue up to enter Gremio
- After watching brainstorm with the students:
- What has just happened?
- What is the major source of conflict between Katherina and Bianca?
- How does Bianca feel about her suitors?
- Baptista clearly prefers Bianca, how does this make Katherina feel?
- Students write a short paragraph answering each of these questions after class discussions.
- Students write additions to the character profiles for the following characters:
- Katherina
- Bianca
- Baptista
- Pack up

Lesson reflection:

Stage: 5   Topic: Act II Scene 1 The Taming of the Shrew   Lesson: 8

Learning Intention: To begin exploring The Taming of the Shrew, understanding the characters, themes and structure of the play.

Teaching strategy: explicit teaching AV material and class discussion towards the creation of notes.

Presentation:
- Settle class and Roll.
- Hand out play script of and rewatch from Petruchio and Katherine's dialogue Act I Scene 2 of The Taming of the Shrew to their exit.
- After watching brainstorm with the students:
- There is a long passage between Petruchio and Katherine here, which is generally considered one of the highlights of the play? Why do you think it is here?
- Why does Petruchio lie to Baptista?
- Katherina stops complaining after Petruchio defends her in front of her father and the other men. Why?
- Why would Petruchio CHOOSE Katherina over a more pliant and subservient wife? What does this tell us about him?
- Students write a short paragraph answering each of these questions after class discussions.
- Students write further details of a character profiles for the following characters:
- Katherina
- Petruchio
- Pack up

Lesson reflection:

Stage: 5   Topic: Act II Scene 1 The Taming of the Shrew   Lesson: 9

Learning Intention: To begin exploring The Taming of the Shrew, understanding the characters, themes and structure of the play.

Teaching strategy: explicit teaching AV material and class discussion towards the creation of notes.

Presentation:
- Settle class and Roll.
- Hand out play script of and watch from the exit of Petruchio and Katherine to the end of the scene Act II Scene 1 of The Taming of the Shrew.
- After watching brainstorm with the students:
- What has just happened?
- How do Tranio and Gremio vie for Bianca?
- Why does Tranio win?
- Do they care about how Bianca feels about all this?
- Students write a short paragraph answering each of these questions after class discussions.
- Students write additions to the character profiles for the following characters:
- Tranio
- Gremio
- Baptista
- Pack up

Lesson reflection:

Stage: 5　　　Topic: Act II The Taming of the Shrew - Themes
Lesson: 10

Learning Intention: To begin exploring The Taming of the Shrew understanding the themes and the structure of the play.

Teaching strategy: explicit teaching and class discussion towards the creation of notes.

Presentation:
- Settle class and Roll.
- Plot lines – Students add to the table in their books under these headings: Bianca & Suitors, Katherina and Petruchio, Lucentio and Tranio. Under each heading put the major plot points that relate to each pairing. This will be a document that the students add to so make sure that they leave enough room for the five acts.
- Themes – Petruchio and Katherina are placed as the authentic characters against the inauthentic qualities of the others. How do we see this in the wooing scene? Petruchio told Hortensio earlier that provided his bride has money he doesn't care how awful she is. Do you think he was telling the truth?
Katherina never receives suitors, is she right to be defensive when she is wooed by Petruchio? How does Petruchio show that he is truly trying to woo her and is not mocking her? How is their verbal sparing a sign that they are well matched?
Students can attach quotes to the theme to back up their predictions.
- Pack up

Lesson reflection:

Stage: 5   **Topic: Act III Scene 1 The Taming of the Shrew**
Lesson: 11

Learning Intention: To begin exploring The Taming of the Shrew, understanding the characters, themes and structure of the play.

Teaching strategy: explicit teaching AV material and class discussion towards the creation of notes.

Presentation:
- Settle class and Roll.
- Hand out play script of and watch Act III Scene 1.
- After watching brainstorm with the students:
- What has just happened?
- Is Bianca as sweet and innocent as she appears from a distance?
- How does this play into the theme of illusion?
- Why is Hortensio disillusioned about Bianca?
- Students write a short paragraph answering each of these questions after class discussions.
- Students write additions to the character profiles for the following characters:
- Bianca
- Hortensio
- Lucentio
- Pack up

Lesson reflection:

Stage: 5   **Topic: Act III Scene 2 The Taming of the Shrew**
Lesson: 12

Learning Intention: To begin exploring The Taming of the Shrew, understanding the characters, themes and structure of the play.

Teaching strategy: explicit teaching AV material and class discussion towards the creation of notes.

Presentation:
- Settle class and Roll.
- Hand out play script of and watch Act III Scene 2 up to the re-entry of Gremio.
- After watching brainstorm with the students:
- What has just happened?
- Katherine didn't even want to get married, so why is she so upset?
- Does Petruchio's appearance make the situation any better?
- What is Petruchio's defence of his appearance?
- Students write a short paragraph answering each of these questions after class discussions.
- Using Biondello's description students are to draw Petruchio.
- Pack up

Lesson reflection:

Stage: 5   Topic: Act III Scene 2 The Taming of the Shrew   Lesson: 13

Learning Intention: To begin exploring The Taming of the Shrew, understanding the characters, themes and structure of the play.

Teaching strategy: explicit teaching AV material and class discussion towards the creation of notes.

Presentation:

- Settle class and Roll.
- Hand out play script of and watch Act III Scene 2 from the re entry of Gremio.
- After watching brainstorm with the students:
- What has just happened?
- Does the situation improve in the church?
- Why do you think this was described rather than shown?
- How does Kate try to control her new husband? Does it work?
- Do we have any idea yet why Petruchio is acting like a maniac?
- How do Katherine's family react?
- Students write a short paragraph answering each of these questions after class discussions.
- Students add to their character profiles of:
- Petruchio
- Katherine
- Baptista
- Pack up

Lesson reflection:

Stage: 5   Topic: Themes in Act III The Taming of the Shrew
Lesson: 14

Learning Intention: To begin exploring Themes in The Taming of the Shrew, understanding the characters, themes and structure of the play.

Teaching strategy: explicit teaching and class discussion towards the creation of notes.

Presentation:
- Settle class and Roll.
- Plot lines – Students add to the table created last theme lesson: Bianca & Suitors, Katherina and Petruchio, Lucentio and Tranio. Under each heading put the major plot points that relate to each pairing.
- Themes
– Individuality vs Conformity

Katherina has submitted to the expectations of her society in fulfilling the role of the Bride. She does not however conform to the ideals of a gentlewoman of her status, so why is she so angry at Petruchio for failing to submit to the expectations of a Groom? Has Petruchio actually shown himself to be conformist in any way in the play so far? What do you think Katerina is actually afraid of? What is she covering with her "Shrewish" behaviour?

- Appearance vs Reality

Bianca plays the game of conforming to the ideals of a gentlewoman in her society. In what ways have we seen that this is not the reality of Bianca? How is she rewarded at the end of the act for her performance? How do the other characters refuse to look deeper than surface appearances? How do Tranio and Lucentio take advantage of this?

- Pack up

Lesson reflection:

Stage: 5   Topic: Act IV Scene 1 The Taming of the Shrew   Lesson: 15

Learning Intention: To begin exploring The Taming of the Shrew, understanding the characters, themes and structure of the play.

Teaching strategy: explicit teaching AV material and class discussion towards the creation of notes.

Presentation:
- Settle class and Roll.
- Hand out play script of and watch Act IV Scene 1.
- After watching brain storm with the students:
- What has just happened?
- Do we have any idea yet why Petruchio is still acting like a maniac?
- How does Kate try to control her new husband? Does it work?
- A trained falcon is the metaphor Petruchio uses to describe "taming" Katherina. Traditionally a falconer is male and the female falcons and hawks are most often used, they form a hunting pair. A trained falcon is not domesticated or submissive, nor is it passive. If he wished for a passive wife he would use the metaphor of a song bird which has to be caged. A falcon is capable of flying free, of essentially running away with no way for a handler to catch it should it wish to leave, but it has bonded with and learnt to trust it's handler. Does Petruchio actually want to break Katherina's spirit or is he after something else?
- Students write a short paragraph answering each of these questions after class discussions.
- Students add to their character profiles of:
- Petruchio
- Katherine
- Grumio
- Pack up

Lesson reflection:

Stage: 5   Topic: Act IV Scene 2 The Taming of the Shrew   Lesson: 16

Learning Intention: To begin exploring The Taming of the Shrew, understanding the characters, themes and structure of the play.

Teaching strategy: explicit teaching AV material and class discussion towards the creation of notes.

Presentation:
- Settle class and Roll.
- Hand out play script of and watch Act IV Scene 2.
- After watching brainstorm with the students:
- What has just happened?
- Why has Hortensio given up on Bianca? What is he going to do now?
- How does Tranio trick the traveller? Why?
- Students write a short paragraph answering each of these questions after class discussions.
- Students add to their character profiles of:
- Lucentio
- Hortensio
- Bianca
- Pack up

Lesson reflection:

Stage: 5   Topic: Act IV Scene 3 The Taming of the Shrew   Lesson: 17

Learning Intention: To begin exploring The Taming of the Shrew, understanding the characters, themes and structure of the play.

Teaching strategy: explicit teaching AV material and class discussion towards the creation of notes.

Presentation:
- Settle class and Roll.
- Hand out play script of and watch Act IV Scene 3.
- After watching brainstorm with the students:
- What has just happened?
- Like a falconer, Petruchio's training is all positive reinforcement. He refuses to reinforce negative behaviour, like tantrum throwing, but offers inducements for positive behaviour. Find two examples of positive reinforcement in this scene.
- How does Petruchio react when Katherina disagrees with him? How does this work to discourage her shrewish behaviour?
- A falcon will wear a blind when not hunting, and thus must trust the falconer to treat her well and keep her safe. Petruchio's speech at the end of the scene talks of the inherent value of things regardless of outward appearance. He asks her to refer anything that she thinks could shame her to him. Does she fully understand his intentions behind what he is saying to her yet?
- Students write a short paragraph answering each of these questions after class discussions.
- Students add to their character profiles of:
- Petruchio
- Katherina
- Hortensio
- Pack up

Lesson reflection:

Stage: 5   Topic: Act IV Scene 4 The Taming of the Shrew   Lesson: 18

Learning Intention: To begin exploring The Taming of the Shrew, understanding the characters, themes and structure of the play.

Teaching strategy: explicit teaching AV material and class discussion towards the creation of notes.

Presentation:
- Settle class and Roll.
- Hand out play script of and watch Act IV Scene 4.
- After watching brainstorm with the students:
- What has just happened?
- Why is Baptista taken in by the pretend father?
- What does this tell us about how Baptista values appearance over authenticity?
- Students write a short paragraph answering each of these questions after class discussions.
- Students add to their character profiles of:
- Lucentio
- Tranio
- Baptista
- Pack up

Lesson reflection:

Stage: 5   Topic: Act IV Scene 5 The Taming of the Shrew   Lesson: 19

Learning Intention: To begin exploring The Taming of the Shrew, understanding the characters, themes and structure of the play.

Teaching strategy: explicit teaching AV material and class discussion towards the creation of notes.

Presentation:

- Settle class and Roll.
- Hand out play script of and watch Act IV Scene 5.
- After watching brainstorm with the students:
- What has just happened?
- Why does Katherina start to play along with Petruchio? How does this fit in with the symbolism of a falconer and falcon working together as a team?
- Who is the traveller they meet? Why is he going to Padua?
- Hortensio believes that he has learned how to "tame" a wife. Do you think he understands the partnership that has developed between Katherine and Petruchio, or has he just seen Petruchio bully her into submission?
- Students write a short paragraph answering each of these questions after class discussions.
- Students add to their character profiles of:
- Petruchio
- Katherina
- Hortensio
- Vincentio
- Pack up

Lesson reflection:

Stage: 5   Topic: Themes in Act IV The Taming of the Shrew
Lesson: 20

Learning Intention: To begin exploring Themes in The Taming of the Shrew, understanding the characters, themes and structure of the play.

Teaching strategy: explicit teaching and class discussion towards the creation of notes.

Presentation:
- Settle class and Roll.
- Plot lines – Students add to the table created last theme lesson: Bianca & Suitors, Katherina and Petruchio, Lucentio and Tranio. Under each heading put the major plot points that relate to each pairing.
- Themes
– Value. What do we value in relationships and why?
Katherina is always defending her worth in the face of constant criticism. How does Petruchio show that he values her as herself? And why is it important for him that she see that he values her?
How does Bianca's value diminish in the eyes of Hortensio? What did he value about her from afar that proved false when viewed up close?
- Trust. Who do we trust in relationships and why?
Petruchio wants Katherina to trust him. Why does she have difficulty trusting anyone?
Does Hortensio trust the rich widow? Or does his desire to learn how to "tame" her suggest that he does not trust her at all? What does this tell us about how he sees the role of a wife?
- This can be discussed and worked on in pairs with reporting back to the whole class.
- Pack up

Lesson reflection:

Stage: 5   Topic: Act V Scene 1 The Taming of the Shrew   Lesson: 21

Learning Intention: To begin exploring The Taming of the Shrew, understanding the characters, themes and structure of the play.

Teaching strategy: explicit teaching AV material and class discussion towards the creation of notes.

Presentation:
- Settle class and Roll.
- Hand out play script of and watch Act V Scene 1.
- After watching brainstorm with the students:
- What has just happened?
- How do the disguises cause chaos?
- How can we see Bianca as a far more scheming character than she first appears?
- Students write a short paragraph answering each of these questions after class discussions.
- Students add to their character profiles of:
- Lucentio
- Bianca
- Baptista
- Vincentio
- Pack up

Lesson reflection:

Stage: 5   Topic: Act V Scene 1 The Taming of the Shrew   Lesson: 22

Learning Intention: To begin exploring The Taming of the Shrew, understanding the characters, themes and structure of the play.

Teaching strategy: explicit teaching AV material and class discussion towards the creation of notes.

Presentation:
- Settle class and Roll.
- Rewatch Act IV Scene 5 focusing on Petruchio and Katherina at the very end of this scene.
- Traditionally comedies end with a wedding, this play has a wedding in the centre of the play and a second at the end. In the 2019 gender swap production Katherina takes his/her wedding ring off and looks at the sun through it in Act IV Scene 5, before returning it and agreeing with Petruchio that it is indeed the moon, symbolising her/his acceptance of their marriage. How does this change the way you can interpret the preceding scenes?
- Kissing seals the joining of two people in a wedding. The last time Petruchio kissed Kate was at the end of their formal wedding ceremony. This time Petruchio asks Kate to kiss him and she agrees, in-spite of it not being conventional. Can we see these two scenes as the end of a second wedding ceremony, this time one between true partners?
- Students write a short paragraph answering each of these questions after class discussions.
- Students add to their character profiles of:
- Petruchio
- Katherina
- Pack up

Lesson reflection:

Stage: 5   Topic: Act V Scene 2 The Taming of the Shrew   Lesson: 23 and 24

Learning Intention: To begin exploring The Taming of the Shrew, understanding the characters, themes and structure of the play.

Teaching strategy: explicit teaching AV material and class discussion towards the creation of notes.

Presentation:
- Settle class and Roll.
- Hand out play script of and watch Act V Scene 2.
- After watching brainstorm with the students:
- What has just happened?
- Why do Lucentio, Hortensio, Bianca and the widow bait Petruchio in this scene?
- What do you think of their attempts to provoke angry behaviour from Katherina?
- How does Katherina actually behave in the face of provocation?
- Are Bianca and the widow as compliant now that they are married?
- When Katherina appears at Petruchio's command he tells her to 'swinge' the other wives from the other room back to where the men are. Swinge means to thrash, beat and flog. Shrews are rodents, and the natural prey of raptors like falcons. How does this exchange show Katherina's evolution as a character.
- Falcons wear caps when not hunting, if we keep with this extended metaphor, how can we see Petruchio's order to throw down her cap?
- Katherina's speech here was considered hackneyed even in Shakespeare's time. Remember he lived under a very powerful and popular female monarch in Elizabeth I. Do you think Shakespeare intended this to be read straight? Or rather is it reminding the women who have been so inauthentic in order to catch a husband that they have to maintain that lie forever now?
- Katherina has helped her husband win a great deal of money and

respect. Again we have a kiss between Katherina and Petruchio and a

reference to actually going to bed. Has she been tamed as the men remark at the end of the play or has she transformed?
- Students write a short paragraph answering each of these questions after class discussions.
- Students add to their character profiles of:
- Lucentio
- Bianca
- Baptista
- Hortensio
- Petruchio
- Katherina
- Pack up

Lesson reflection:

Stage: 5 **Topic:** Act V The Taming of the Shrew - Themes **Lesson:** 25

Learning Intention: To begin exploring The Taming of the Shrew understanding the themes and the structure of the play.

Teaching strategy: explicit teaching and class discussion towards the creation of notes.

Presentation:
- Settle class and Roll.
- Plot lines – Students draw up a table in their books with these headings: Bianca & Suitors, Katherina and Petruchio, Lucentio and Tranio. Under each heading put the major plot points that relate to each pairing. This will be a document that the students add to so make sure that they leave enough room for the five acts.
- Themes – Transformation.

 Katherina and Bianca both transform over the course of this play. Katherina's transformation is far more obvious and forms the main plot of the play, from unloved and disregarded "Shrew" to valued and loved partner. Bianca also undergoes a transformation, which is more subtle and less often remarked upon. What seems an abrupt change in her character in Act V is actually signposted through out the play. In fact Bianca's "Descent" into a shewish wife can be mapped against Katherina's rise to respected partner.
- Look back over Bianca's scenes and chart her transformation from a "blank" to a woman with a character of her own.
- Why do you think Bianca hid her own "shrewish" nature until after she had secured a husband?
- Students write a short paragraph answering each of these questions after class discussions using their own words with details.
- Students share their individual responses in a class discussion.
- Pack up

Lesson reflection:

Essay Writing Lessons

Year 10 Unit.

Stage: 5   Topic: Essay writing introduction   Lesson: 26

Learning Intention: Students learn how to unpack an essay question so that they can answer it in the most effective manner.

Teaching strategy: Explicit teaching centred instruction, class discussion and student centred work.

Presentation:

- Settle class and Roll.
- Introduce to students that we are going to be spending the next five lessons on essay writing as the conclusion of the unit. And hand out the essay question for whichever play you have studied.

Julius Caesar – The word 'Love' is used more times in <u>Julius Caesar</u> than in any other of Shakespeare's plays. Examine how Love in its many forms can be seen as the motivating factor behind the characters actions in this play.

The Taming of the Shrew – <u>The Taming of the Shrew</u> is a play about disguise and transformation. Compare and contrast the use of disguise and transformation by the Minola sisters across the course of the play.

Henry IV Part 1 – <u>In Henry IV Part 1</u> Hal and Hotspur have very different definitions of honour and duty. Examine how this brings about the various conflicts throughout the play.

- Have students circle what they think are the most important words in the question. Copy the question onto the board and circle the underlined text. Explain to the students that when reading an essay question they should be looking for:
- Who they need to focus on.
- Where their focus should be.

- How they should approach the question.

Julius Caesar – The word 'Love' is used more times in Julius Caesar than in any other of Shakespeare's plays. <u>Examine</u> how <u>Love</u> in its many forms can be seen as the <u>motivating factor behind</u> the <u>character's actions</u> in this play.

The Taming of the Shrew – The Taming of the Shrew is a play about disguise and transformation. <u>Compare</u> and <u>contrast</u> the use of <u>disguise</u> and <u>transformation</u> by the <u>Minola sisters</u> across the course of the play.

Henry IV Part 1 – In Henry IV Part 1 <u>Hal and Hotspur</u> have very <u>different definitions</u> of <u>honour</u> and <u>duty</u>. <u>Examine</u> how this brings about the <u>various conflicts</u> throughout the play.

- What do the verbs mean?

Examine – Present in depth and investigate the significance of the thing being examined.
Compare - Identify the characteristics or qualities two or more things have in common.
Contrast – Point out the difference between two things.

- Hand out worksheet and have students fill in for their respective question. Make sure that students include quotes or examples from the play.
- Pack up
Lesson reflection:

Henry IV Part 1 - **Fill in for** Hal and Hotspur	
Duty to family:	
Duty to country:	
Duty to friends:	
Honour as an abstract notion:	
Honour as a personal code:	

Julius Caesar - Fill in for Brutus, Marc Antony and Cassius	
Love of country:	
Love of friend:	
Love of freedom:	
Love of integrity:	

The Taming of the Shrew - Fill in for Bianca and Katherine	
Authentic self:	
Disguises adopted:	
Transformation performed:	

Stage: 5	Topic: Essay planning	Lesson: 27

Learning Intention: To learn how to structure and plan an essay.

Teaching strategy: Explicit teaching centred instruction, class discussion and student centred work.

Presentation:
- Settle class and Roll.
- Hand out essay structure sheet.

Brainstorm with the class the following questions:
- What are the most significant structural features?
- Word Count
- Formal register
- Depth and complexity of argument
- Logical flow of ideas
- How to use, attribute and lay out quotes
- Hand out sample essay to students.
- Read through the essay and discuss what makes it a top mark essay.

Look particularly at:
- Structure
- Language choices
- Choice of evidence and what constitutes evidence e.g. direct quotes and examples from the play. And how are they different.
- Use of quotations and correct citation and formatting.
- Word count and why you don't count quotes in your 850 words.
- Formal language worksheet
- Pack up

Lesson reflection:

How to lay out an essay.

Introduction.
This is where you break down the question and introduce how you plan to tackle the answer. This is not the place to start answering the question. 100 words maximum

First body paragraph.
This is where you outline your argument for the statement made in the question. If the question is a compare and contrast essay question this is where you would examine the compare aspect. 200 words maximum

Second body paragraph.
This is where you outline your argument against or raise objections to the statement made in the question. If the question is a compare and contrast essay question this is where you would examine the contrast aspect. 200 words maximum

Third body paragraph.
This is the most important part of your essay, this is where you will flesh out your argument with quotes. Quotes provide stronger evidence than examples. This is where you take a definite side and argue it. You can take a position that argues against the question. Or one that supports the statement made in the question. Or that is implied in the question. 300 words approx

Conclusion.
Like the introduction, you are not introducing new information, but summing up your argument. This does not need to be long. 50 – 100 words.

Word count.
The word count of your essay is 850 words. It is generally accepted practice that you can write + or – 10% so 85 words and receive no penalty. More words is not a virtue in and of itself if it does not add to your argument. It is best to aim for as close to your word count as possible rather than falling short. If your essay has fallen short by a long way, then it means that your argument is weak and it would be worth going back and looking for places where it can be strengthened or expanded.

Quotes are not counted in the word count. This allows you to have the maximum number of words to make your argument. While at the same time allowing you to use longer quotes without penalty.

If typed, quotes should be italicised.

Quotes should always start on a new line and your essay should pick up on a new line. You will see how this works in the sample essay in a moment.

Formal language.
An essay is a formal piece of writing. It is a piece that is always written in the third person. This gives it an authoritative quality. You are making an argument and showing off what you have learned. The implied reader of an essay is reading it to learn

something. So while it is acceptable to assume their knowledge of the topic and you don't need to recap the plot, they are reading to find out how you argue the question. The depth of your answer and the formality of you language shows respect for the reader.

Your argument should be logical, backed up by evidence and flow. One argument should build upon another until you reach your conclusion. Feel free to show examples that come from across the text. This will show that you are familiar with the material and know your subject.

Linking words to create formal register

Words to use instead of: Also, As well and Too.	Likewise Correspondingly Equally Not only... but also In the same way Similarly	
Words to use instead of: So and Because.	Consequently As a result Thus Since Therefore Accordingly This suggests that	It follows that For this reason
Words to use instead of: But, Yet, and Still.	Alternatively However Conversely Instead On the contrary Despite/in spite of While (not whilst!)	Nevertheless Nonetheless Although Admittedly Even so On the contrary
Words to use instead of: I think.	To illustrate To clarify Further (not 'furthermore') First, second and third (not firstly, secondly and thirdly) For instance	Especially In fact Namely In addition Moreover Typically
Words to use instead of: In conclusion.	To summarise It can be concluded that As can be seen Ultimately Given the above As described Finally	

Henry IV is accused of being a cunning politician, by Hotspur. Consider how Hal is not only a greater, but a subtler politician than his father.

King Henry IV, often referred to as Bolingbroke, is in the estimation of Henry Percy, or Hotspur, a cunning politician and not a true king. It is this hobby horse of Hotspur's that leads him and his family and allies into conflict with King Henry over the course of this play. While it is not a source of contention that King Henry is an astute political actor throughout the play, it is less obvious that his son Prince Henry, or Hal, is equally astute in his maintenance of a public persona and can be argued is a greater and more subtle politician than his father. Not only in how he manages his role as Prince of Wales, but also how he maintains his popular image making allies rather than enemies as he travels through the world of the play.

Henry IV Part 1 is a play that examines what makes a king legitimate, and whether legitimacy as a king is inherited or taken through possession of the crown itself. This is the central dilemma that plagues the titular character, Henry IV. The opening of the play brings the audience a kingdom beset by rebellion on its borders and ruled by a king who is insecure about his position, resolved to travel to Jerusalem as soon as possible to make penance for his dispossession of the former king, Richard II. In this act we see the first sign of the subtle politician, his penitent attitude subordinate to both the needs of the state, threats from abroad, and to his personal desire to remain king. The penance of the king is a political act as much as a personal. It enhances his image before his supporters and differentiates him from the image of the usurping tyrant. Henry IV exploits this image as a strong protector of the kingdom with the reluctant ruler throughout the play, emphasising his self sacrifice as a way of maintaining power. He is holding on to his power, by maintaining the charade that he never desired it in the first place.

Prince Henry, or Hal, unlike his father is not burdened with the question of whether his claim to the crown would be legitimate, as his coronation would see the restoration of primogenitor and the beginning of a new line of kings. Hal's expression of his greater political subtlety comes in his careful manipulation of his image. The opening of the play presents the audience with the image of a wild and irresponsible young prince, upon whom the future health of the kingdom relies. The king openly disparages his own son before the court and he is viewed with contempt by Henry Percy. Hal spends his time drinking and rough housing with low born reprobates and neglects his place in court. However, this is merely part of Hal's subtle plan, to gain respect, legitimacy and love that his father had never manage to derive from both nobles and commoners alike.

It is easiest to see these distinctions between father and son when we look at how they handle similar situations. First, special requests. In the opening of the play Hotspur, requests that his brother-in-law Mortimer, be ransomed from Glendower. Mortimer was named heir by deposed Richard II and is a sensitive subject for the King. His response to Hotspur's request is,
"No, on the barren mountain let him starve;/ for I shall never hold that man my friend/

Whose tongue shall ask me for one penny cost/ To ransom home revolted Mortimer." Henry IV Part 1 Act I Scene 3.

This response helps to foment Hotspur's revolt against the King. Conversely, when Falstaff in the Act IV play makes an impossible request of Hal, in expectation of significant power and influence over the future king. Hal manages to both negotiate a refusal and maintain his relationship with his friend, by playacting as his father.

"FALSTAFF…banish not him form thy Harry's company: banish plump Jack and banish all the world.

"PRINCE I do. I will." Henry IV Part 1 Act II Scene 4.

Second, public image is contrasted between father and son, with Hal arguably again surpassing his father in his subtlety. In the great dressing down of Hal that the King gives in Act 3 Scene 2 Henry IV describes himself as:

"By being seldom seen. I could not stir/ but, like a comet, I was wondered at:" Henry IV Part 1 Act III Scene 2.

In the same speech Henry compares his son to deposed Richard II:

"He was but as the cuckoo is in June,/ Heard, but not regarded….And in that very very line, Harry, stand'st though;" Henry IV Part 1 Act III Scene 2.

However, Hal is acutely aware of his current public image, having chosen to present himself in a dissipated style, though one more in appearance than in fact as can be seen in his opening monologue:

"My reformation, glittering o'er my fault,/ Shall show more goodly and attract more eyes/ Than that which has no foil to set it off." Henry IV Part 1 Act I Scene 2.

This faith that Hal has in his ability to transform his public image is vindicated in the final act of the play, where his embodiment of the loyal son, subject and Prince is so complete that even Vernon, a member of the rebellion, is moved twice to praise him:

"I saw young Harry with his beaver on/ His cushes on his thighs, gallantly arm'd,/ Rise from the ground like feathered Mercury,/ And vaulted with such ease into his seat/ As if an angel dropp'd down from the clouds/ To turn and wind a fiery Pegasus/ And witch the world with noble horsemanship." Henry IV Part 1 Act IV Scene 1.

And again after he has offered single combat with Hotspur to resolve the conflict:

"No, by my soul. I never in my life/ Did hear a challenge urg'd more modestly,/ Unless a brother should a brother dare/ To gentle exercise and proof of arms." Henry IV Part 1 Act V Scene 2.

By the end of the play when Hal claims his title as Prince of Wales, neither the audience nor the other characters on the stage are in any doubt as to his deserving of that role.

Hal proves that he is a more masterful politician than his father through not only his ability to win and hold friends, but in his ability win over also the admiration of his enemies. Hal commands a respect that his father struggled to hold, even with the trapping of kingship. Henry IV conversely had been unable to manipulate his public image. Sticking instead to a single remote image that had served him well when he was a challenger to the former King, but which failed to negotiate the complex relationships within the court, losing him the respect of powerful allies. Thus when Hal claims his full title, we see a young man who can skilfully negotiate power and respect, which ultimately makes him the more skilled politician.

Word count 919 words + 246 in quotes

At the end of the play Antony calls Brutus "the noblest Roman of them all." Examine how Brutus embodies the nobility of Rome and how this guides his actions throughout the play.

Marc Antony's lines at the end of Julius Caesar are meant to be flattering and complementary to his fallen enemy Marcus Brutus. Investing in him no malice, but only the purest of motives in his part in the assassination of Caesar. This is a fitting tribute to a tragic hero. However, how can a man moved by only the purest and most noble motive commit a treasonous act of killing a head of state? It can be argued in fact, that those very noble motives left Brutus open to manipulation and his final tragic death. Nobility of mind and action are no shield against manipulation and political pragmatism.

Brutus' claims to nobility are multi-faceted. First, he is a member of a Roman family who traces their lineage back to before the overthrow of the tyrant king Tarquin and the founding of the Roman republic. A lineage that he is himself proud of and others respect. Second, his idealism and belief in the ideal of Rome and his loyalty to that belief, make him a solid and dependable individual. One who will act from collective interest rather than self-seeking ones. Finally, there is his reason and his ability to think things through logically and coldly, never acting on impulse. These traits are strengths in Brutus' character and win him the admiration of other characters in the play.

Conversely, it can be argued that these very traits that lead Brutus to be admired for his nobility, contain the seeds of his ultimate tragic end. Brutus' keen sense of his family heritage and the important role his ancestor played in the founding of the Republic, create in him a sense of inferiority. It is an insecurity that Cassius sees and exploits explicitly. The idealism of Brutus also causes him to act in ways that are at best described as politically naive. Assuming that everyone around him shares his idealism, leads Brutus to underestimate and blindly trust the words of more politically astute players. Finally, the cold, rational and logical approach to problems leaves Brutus blind to the power of emotion as a weapon and to the motives and reactions of others around him.

Is Brutus a noble individual? Yes. Does that nobility leave him open to manipulation and deceit causing his downfall? Also yes. The Rome of Julius Caesar is very far from the Rome of Brutus' lofty ideals. The play opens with a victorious Caesar entering Rome having defeated Pompey and ending the civil wars. This state of affairs has left many in Rome discontent. The Tribunes scold the people for celebrating Caesar as wildly as they once celebrated his defeated rival Pompey. While Cassius, not in favour with Caesar, is plotting against him, as he says:

"Caesar doth bear me hard, but he loves Brutus." Julius Caesar Act I Scene 2

And Caesar himself says:

"Such men as he be never at heart's ease/ Whiles they behold a greater than themselves,/ And therefore are they very dangerous." Julius Caesar Act I Scene 2

In contrast Brutus contemplates how far Rome has fallen from the ideal that he holds of it, and seeks a remedy to restore his idealised vision.

"Brutus had rather be a villager/ Than to repute himself a son of Rome/ under these hard

conditions as this time/ Is like to lay upon us." Julius Caesar Act I Scene 2

Brutus' joining of the conspiracy is thus naive and this leaves him open to manipulation. In fact it is his very nobility that Cassius is counting on to sway him to his side.

"Well, Brutus, that art noble; yet I see,/ Thy honourable metal may be wrought/ From that it is disopos'd:" Julius Caesar Act I Scene 2

Cassius uses reference to Brutus' ancestor in anonymous notes precisely because he knows that he must appeal to honourable motives, rather than personal gain. He also knows that he can firm up the support of his fellow conspirators, by bringing the highly respected Brutus into the conspiracy.

Brutus' political idealism does not cause him to question the motives of any of the other conspirators, a trait that Cassius is acutely aware of.

"If I were Brutus now, and he were Cassius,/ he should not humour me." Julius Caesar Act I Scene 2

Nor does Brutus see beyond the surface of others, as he councils that Antony be left untouched in the assassination, and even allows Antony to speak at Caesar's funeral oration. Dismissing Antony as merely a drunken rioter, and failing to see the calculating politician and masterful General beneath the public image.

Perhaps his greatest failing, however is his logical and rational mind that fails to grasp the use of emotion as a weapon. Brutus' justification for the assassination of Caesar is delivered to the people in prose, using appeals to logic, which the crowd misunderstand as they offer Brutus the crown they had previously offered Caesar. Antony in contrast, offers a much stronger speech, without once uttering an overtly negative statement against the conspirators nor offering a single logical or rational reason for the assassination to be condemned. Instead he speaks verse and plays upon the emotions of the crowd, showing the bloodied robes and body of Caesar. Turning the crowd against Brutus, whom they were so ready moments ago to crown.

The play Julius Caesar is the tragedy of the fall of the noblest of the Romans, Marcus Brutus. The irony of the play is that it is the very nobility for which he his praised in the closing lines, that ultimately causes his downfall. Brutus is noble, but his nobility left him vulnerable to manipulation, blind to the reality of situations and individuals, which was apparent to everyone else, and easy prey to the more astute and subtle political operators who surrounded him. In some ways it can be argued that Brutus was too noble to survive in the ignoble world of Shakespeare's Rome.

867 words +121 in quotes

Examine Shakespeare's use of animal imagery throughout the play. How do these descriptions and extended metaphors contribute to the audience's understanding of The Taming of the Shrew?

The use of animal imagery is integral to the audience's understanding of The Taming of the Shrew. Animal imagery is evoked in crucial scene within the play and these images, rather than providing mere verbal decoration are tropes that run through the play highlighting characters and their journey of transformation. The most crucial of these images being those of the Shrew, a small mouse like mammal generally seen as a pest. And falcons, the female bird used in the noble sport of falconry, a form of hunting performed by a man and bird team. These two powerful images are offset by the frequent references to other animals that will also be discussed.

A shrew is a small mouse like animal that preys upon insects and is aggressively territorial. They possess sharp teeth and emit a pungent odour. In Shakespeare's England, a shrew was a colloquial term for an aggressive and disagreeable woman. The term shrew, with this latter meaning is applied to Katherina Minola, making her the titular character in this play. And while Katherina is the titular character, she is so in a way which entirely dehumanises her. The audience is introduced to both Katherina and Bianca as their father attempts to offer his elder daughter Katherina to the suitors of his younger, Bianca. Katherina, feeling that she is being offered as a consolation prize, complains that her father's offer makes her a prostitute. While the suitors, object that Katherina is too wild and aggressive to make an appropriate wife. This dehumanisation of being likened to a shrew, undermines Katherina's real and obvious objections to being treated as second class to her bland and thus more desirable younger sister.

The image of the falcon and the discussion of falconry, gives a second image for Katherina to play within. The imagery of the falcon, does not occur until after Katherina's marriage to Petruchio. Their courtship scene enabled both to battle wits in likening the other to various animals, it is clear that neither hits upon an image that sticks, each animal rolling off their backs as they reach for another simile to progress the engagement. The imagery of the falcon, however becomes an extended metaphor for the remainder of the play, giving Katherina a new role to evolve into.

The use of animal imagery is deliberately chosen to show the relative powerlessness of the female characters in relation to the men in the play. Marriage bargains are negotiated between father's and prospective bridegrooms, with the wooing of the women as a mere formality. Once married the bride is her husband's property, as Petruchio says:
"I will be master of what is mine own./ She is my goods, my chattels; she is my house,/ my household stuff, my field, my barn, / my horse, my ox, my ass, my anything;" The Taming of the Shrew Act III Scene 2
If women are to be regarded as nothing but property, then it is only natural that they should be dehumanised to the level of animal, in Katherina's case a shrew, something of no value, which only causes harm to property. Bianca, for all her admiration, is no less dehumanised by the praise heaped on her, as she becomes a jewel, or one of many

possible Roman goddesses. In other words, a thing to be treasured.

The use of falcons and falconry offers a different potential marital relationship, than the simple possession and prize dynamic of the dehumanised trophy like Bianca. In the battle of wills that constitutes the "taming" aspect of the play, Petruchio offers a different dynamic to his bride. That of co-hunter. The "taming" that Petruchio engages in is less about breaking the natural instincts of his new wife, as to create a bond of trust between the two of them, as between a falcon and her handler.

"Thus have I politicly begun my reign,/ And 'tis my hope to end successfully./ My falcon now is sharp and passing empty./ ... To make her come, and know her keeper's call," The Taming of the Shrew Act IV Scene 2

While this arrangement appears to be completely to Petruchio's advantage, in trusting and bonding to her new husband, Petruchio makes it clear that he will defend Katherina's honour and dignity. Something that no one, not even her father has done for her in the play so far.

"If thou account'st it shame, lay it on me;" The Taming of the Shrew Act III Scene 2

The value of this defence is seen again in the last scene in the play, where the widow, Bianca, Tranio, and even Baptista, failing to see a submissive Katherina, continue to revile her as a shrew. When Petruchio in his wife's absence proposes the wager on who has the most obedient wife, he does so knowing that Katherina trusts him not to humiliate her and to defend her. Thus her seeming 'obedience', at responding to his order, is not that of a 'tamed' shrew, but of a co-hunter. Shown when Petruchio removes her cap and sends her on the attack.

"Katherine, that cap of yours becomes you not:/ off with that bauble, throw it under foot./ ... Katherine, I charge thee, tell these headstrong women/ What duty they do owe their lords and husbands." The Taming of the Shrew Act V Scene 2.

In this scene Petruchio and Katerina show that they have become the bonded co-hunters, and they are the ones who retire happily to bed, leaving the newly weds perplexed and in discord in their wake.

The animal imagery present throughout The Taming of the Shrew is more than mere decoration. It shows both the deep dehumanisation and humiliation of Katherina as she struggles to assert her person-hood in the humiliating marriage market, where she is seen as less valuable than her compliant sister. It provides an engaging verbal frisson to the sparing/wooing of Petruchio and Katherina. And finally it offers a point of transformation and elevation for Katherina, as she accepts and grows into her role as a wife and companion to her respectful and trusted husband.

868 words +146 quotes

Stage: 5   **Topic: Essay Planning 2**   **Lesson: 28**

Learning Intention: To learn how to structure and plan and essay.

Teaching strategy: Explicit teaching centred instruction and student centred work.

Presentation:
- Settle class and Roll.
- Hand out essay plan template and have students plan their essay in preparation for writing it in the final two lessons.
- Provide students with feedback or assistance on their plan as required.
- Pack up

Lesson reflection:

Julius Caesar – The word 'Love' is used more times in Julius Caesar than in any other of Shakespeare's plays. Examine how Love in its many forms can be seen as the motivating factor behind the characters actions in this play.

Essay plan	
Introduction	
First Body	
Second Body	
Third Body	
Conclusion	

The Taming of the Shrew – The Taming of the Shrew is a play about disguise and transformation. Compare and contrast the use of disguise and transformation by the Minola sisters across the course of the play.

Essay plan	
Introduction	
First Body	
Second Body	
Third Body	
Conclusion	

Henry IV Part 1 – Hal and Hotspur have very different definitions of honour and duty. Examine how this brings about the various conflicts throughout the play.

Essay plan	
Introduction	
First Body	
Second Body	
Third Body	
Conclusion	

Stage: 5	Topic: Essay writing	Lesson: 29 and 30

Learning Intention: Students work on their essays.

Teaching strategy: Student centred learning.

Presentation:

- Settle class and Roll.
- Students are given the two final lessons to write their essays, using the notes and plans that they have developed. This is not an exam, but and essay written in class time. Students can either write their essays by hand or on computer depending on the resources available. Essays must be handed in at the end of the second lesson for their unit grade.
- Pack up

Lesson reflection:

Close reading of a Shakespeare play essay

Curriculum outcomes:
   • Review, edit and refine students' own and others' texts for control of content, organisation, sentence structure, vocabulary, and/or visual features to achieve particular purposes and effects

   • Understand conventions for citing others, and how to reference these in different ways

   • Reflect on, extend, endorse or refute others' interpretations of and responses to literature
      - determining, through debate, whether a text possesses universal qualities and remains relevant
   • Identify and explore the purposes and effects of different text structures and language features of spoken texts, and use this knowledge to create purposeful texts that inform, persuade and engage

The Task:

850 word essay + essay plan answering the following question -

Julius Caesar – The word 'Love' is used more times in Julius Caesar than in any other of Shakespeare's plays. Examine how Love in its many forms can be seen as the motivating factor behind the characters actions in this play.

The Taming of the Shrew – The Taming of the Shrew is a play about disguise and transformation. Compare and contrast the use of disguise and transformation by the Minola sisters across the course of the play.

Henry IV Part 1 – In Henry IV Part 1 Hal and Hotspur have very different definitions of honour and duty. Examine how this brings about the various conflicts throughout the play. (Copy the appropriate question in for your class.)

Success criteria:

Your essay will be marked on how well you:
- Form and state a thesis/ opinion.
- Shows evidence of planning and preperation.
- Flow and logic of your argument.
- Use of formal register language.
- Selection of evidence and quotes to show a through knowledge of the text and support

your argument.
- Follow the stylistic rules of essay writing and layout.

*© Australian Curriculum, Assessment and Reporting Authority (ACARA) 2010 to present, unless otherwise indicated. This material was downloaded from the Australian Curriculum website (www.australiancurriculum.edu.au) (Website) (accessed 13 April 2023) and [was][was not] modified. The material is licensed under CC BY 4.0 (https://creativecommons.org/licenses/by/4.0). Version updates are tracked in the 'Curriculum version history' section on the 'About the Australian Curriculum' page (http://australiancurriculum.edu.au/about-the-australian-curriculum/) of the Australian Curriculum website.

ACARA does not endorse any product that uses the Australian Curriculum or make any representations as to the quality of such products. Any product that uses material published on this website should not be taken to be affiliated with ACARA or have the sponsorship or approval of ACARA. It is up to each person to make their own assessment of the product, taking into account matters including, but not limited to, the version number and the degree to which the materials align with the content descriptions and achievement standards (where relevant). Where there is a claim of alignment, it is important to check that the materials align with the content descriptions and achievement standards (endorsed by all education Ministers), not the elaborations (examples provided by ACARA).

Marking Criteria:

35-29 Exceptional -
- Has fully and thoroughly understood the question and has provided a logical and well reasoned argument.
- Student has planned in detail and has used their plan to help with the construction of the essay.
- The essay takes a strong position and argues it to a logical conclusion.
- Language choices are sophisticated, appropriate to the register and shows respect to the reader.
- Has chosen strong evidence and quotes from the text to back up arguments succinctly and clearly.
- The essay follows the structure and style that was studied as part of the unit. Word count is on point or within the 10% margin. Quotes are on a separate line, and clearly referenced.

28–22 Accomplished -
- Has a clear understanding of the question and has provided a logical argument.
- Student has clearly planned their position and has used their plan to help with the construction of the essay.
- The essay takes a position and argues it to a logical conclusion.
- Language is appropriate to the register and shows respect to the reader.
- Has chosen appropriate evidence and quotes from the text to back up arguments clearly.
- The essay follows the structure and style that was studied as part of the unit. Word count is on point or within the 10% margin. Quotes are on a separate line, and clearly referenced.

21-15 Proficient -
- Has mostly understood the question and has tries to provide a reasoned argument.
- Student has planned. Has included quotes and evidence in their plan and has used their plan to help with the construction of the essay.
- The essay lacks focus and detail, but still argues it to a conclusion.
- Language is mostly appropriate to the register and shows awareness of the reader.
- Has provided evidence and quotes from the text to back up arguments, but not all are appropriate to either the question or argument being made.
- The essay mostly follows the structure and style that was studied as part of the unit. Word count is more than or less than the 10% margin. Quotes are included within the body text, but still identified with quotation marks and clearly referenced.

14-8 Developing -
- Has basic understanding of the question and has provided an argument.
- Student has not planned in any detail. Has no or few quotes or evidence in their plan and has not used their plan to help with the construction of the essay.
- The essay lacks focus and detail, it struggles to draw a conclusion and veers into recount.
- Language is inappropriate to the register and is difficult to follow. Shows little awareness of the reader.
- Has provided little evidence and quotes from the text to back up arguments. Quotes may be well off topic.
- The essay tries to follows the structure and style that was studied as part of the unit. Word count is well over or under the 10% margin. Quotes are included within the body text, not identified with quotation marks and not referenced.

7-0 Elementary -
- Has not understood the question and has provided no argument.
- Student has not planned and has not used their plan to help with the construction of the essay.
- The essay does not address the question in any way, it struggles to draw a conclusion and is mostly recount.
- Language is inappropriate to the register, words are misused and is difficult to follow. Shows no awareness of the reader.
- Has provided no evidence and quotes from the text to back up arguments.
- The essay does not follow the structure and style that was studied as part of the unit. Word count is significantly less than the 850 words required. Quotes not included.

Score   /35

Curriculum Outcomes	Teaching, Learning and Assessment	Resources
Identify and evaluate devices that create tone, for example humour, wordplay, innuendo and parody in poetry, humorous prose, drama or visual texts	Lesson 14 Word play and Puns Lesson 16 Insults Lesson 18 Categories - Comedy	Shaking Up Shakespeare Natalie Muller 2023 Black Cockie Press Notes, playscripts and worksheets.
Interpret and analyse language choices, including sentence patterns, dialogue, imagery and other language features, in short stories, literary essays and plays	Lesson 12-16 "I don't understand what they're saying." Lessons 17-20 Categories, Comedy, history and Tragedy. Lessons 22-24 Persuading the audience	
Recognise, explain and analyse the ways literary texts draw on readers' knowledge of other texts and enable new understanding and appreciation of aesthetic qualities	Lesson 1 Shakespeare? Lesson 2 Is Shakespeare for everyone? Lesson 3 How has Shakespeare changed over time? Lesson 11 Shakespeare the reader Lesson 12 "I don't understand what they're saying." Language	
Create literary texts that draw upon text structures and language features of other texts for particular purposes and effects	Lesson 8&9 Not a lone Genius, but one of many. Lessons 25-30 Shakespeare board game.	
Recognise that vocabulary choices contribute to the specificity, abstraction and style of texts	Lesson 14 Word play and Puns Lesson 16 Insults Lessons17-20 Categories, Comedy, history and Tragedy. Lessons 22-24 Persuading the audience	

Curriculum Outcomes	Teaching, Learning and Assessment	Resources
Share, reflect on, clarify and evaluate opinions and arguments about aspects of literary texts	Lessons 1-30	Shaking Up Shakespeare Natalie Muller 2023 Black Cockie Press Notes, playscripts and worksheets.
Recognise and explain differing viewpoints about the world, cultures, individual people and concerns represented in texts	Lesson 3 How has Shakespeare changed over time? Lesson 4 Shakespeare's Background Lesson 5 The Elizabethan theatre Lesson 6 Becoming an actor Lesson 7 Upstart Crow - Shakespeare appears!	
Apply increasing knowledge of vocabulary, text structures and language features to understand the content of texts	Lessons 12-16 "I don't understand what they're saying." Lessons 22-24 Persuading the audience Lessons 25-30 Shakespeare board game	

© Australian Curriculum, Assessment and Reporting Authority (ACARA) 2010 to present, unless otherwise indicated. This material was downloaded from the Australian Curriculum website (www.australiancurriculum.edu.au) (Website) (accessed 13 April 2023) and was not modified. The material is licensed under CC BY 4.0 (https://creativecommons.org/licenses/by/4.0). Version updates are tracked in the 'Curriculum version history' section on the 'About the Australian Curriculum' page (http://australiancurriculum.edu.au/about-the-australian-curriculum/) of the Australian Curriculum website.

ACARA does not endorse any product that uses the Australian Curriculum or make any representations as to the quality of such products. Any product that uses material published on this website should not be taken to be affiliated with ACARA or have the sponsorship or approval of ACARA. It is up to each person to make their own assessment of the product, taking into account matters including, but not limited to, the version number and the degree to which the materials align with the content descriptions and achievement standards (where relevant). Where there is a claim of alignment, it is important to check that the materials align with the content descriptions and achievement standards (endorsed by all education Ministers), not the elaborations (examples provided by ACARA).

Curriculum Outcomes	Teaching, Learning and Assessment	Resources
Compare and evaluate a range of representations of individuals and groups in different historical, social and cultural contexts - exploring and reflecting on personal experience gained from interpreting literature drawn from cultures and times different from the students' own	Lessons 2 - 25 Henry IV Part 1 Lessons 2-25 Julius Caesar Lessons 2-25 The Taming of the Shrew	Shaking Up Shakespeare Natalie Muller 2023 Black Cockie Press Notes, playscripts and worksheets.
Analyse and evaluate how people, cultures, places, events, objects and concepts are represented in texts, including media texts, through language, structural and/or visual choices	Lessons 1-4, 6-13, 16-18, and 21-24 Henry IV Part 1 Lessons 1-4, 6-10, 12-14, 17-18, and 21-23 Julius Caesar Lessons 1-4, 6-9, 11-13, 15-19, and 21-24 The Taming of the Shrew	
Identify and analyse implicit or explicit values, beliefs and assumptions in texts and how these are influenced by purposes and likely audiences	Lessons 5, 14-15, 19-20 and 25 Henry IV Part 1 Lessons 5, 11,15-16, 19-20 and 24-25 Julius Caesar Lessons 5, 10, 14, 20 and 25 The Taming of the Shrew	
Use comprehension strategies to compare and contrast information within and between texts, identifying and analysing embedded perspectives, and evaluating supporting evidence	Lessons 1-4, 6-13, 16-18, and 21-24 Henry IV Part 1 Lessons 1-4, 6-10, 12-14, 17-18, and 21-23 Julius Caesar Lessons 1-4, 6-9, 11-13, 15-19, and 21-24 The Taming of the Shrew	

Curriculum Outcomes	Teaching, Learning and Assessment	Resources
Reflect on, extend, endorse or refute others' interpretations of and responses to literature – determining, through debate, whether a text possesses universal qualities and remains relevant	Lessons 2-30 Henry IV Part 1 Lessons 2-30 Julius Caesar Lessons 2-30 The Taming of the Shrew	Shaking Up Shakespeare Natalie Muller 2023 Black Cockie Press Notes, playscripts and worksheets.
Review, edit and refine students' own and others' texts for control of content, organisation, sentence structure, vocabulary, and/or visual features to achieve particular purposes and effects	Lessons 26-30 Henry IV Part 1 Lessons 26-30 Julius Caesar Lessons 26-30 The Taming of the Shrew	
Understand conventions for citing others, and how to reference these in different ways	Lessons 1 and 26-30 Henry IV Part 1 Lessons 1 and 26-30 Julius Caesar Lessons 1 and 26-30 The Taming of the Shrew	
Identify and explore the purposes and effects of different text structures and language features of spoken texts, and use this knowledge to create purposeful texts that inform, persuade and engage	Lessons 26-30 Henry IV Part 1 Lessons 26-30 Julius Caesar Lessons 26-30 The Taming of the Shrew	

© Australian Curriculum, Assessment and Reporting Authority (ACARA) 2010 to present, unless otherwise indicated. This material was downloaded from the Australian Curriculum website (www.australiancurriculum.edu.au) (Website) (accessed 13 April 2023) and was not modified. The material is licensed under CC BY 4.0 (https://creativecommons.org/licenses/by/4.0). Version updates are tracked in the 'Curriculum version history' section on the 'About the Australian Curriculum' page (http://australiancurriculum.edu.au/about-the-australian-curriculum/) of the Australian Curriculum website.

ACARA does not endorse any product that uses the Australian Curriculum or make any representations as to the quality of such products. Any product that uses material published on this website should not be taken to be affiliated with ACARA or have the sponsorship or approval of ACARA. It is up to each person to make their own assessment of the product, taking into account matters including, but not limited to, the version number and the degree to which the materials align with the content descriptions and achievement standards (where relevant). Where there is a claim of alignment, it is important to check that the materials align with the content descriptions and achievement standards (endorsed by all education Ministers), not the elaborations (examples provided by ACARA).

Bibliography

Astington, John H. *Actors and Acting in Shakespeare's Time.* Cambridge University Press, 30 Sept. 2010.

Crystal, David, and Ben Crystal. *Shakespeare's Words : A Glossary and Language Companion.* London, Penguin, 2004.

Forse, James H. *Art Imitates Business.* Popular Press, 1993.

Garber, Marjorie B. *Shakespeare after All.* New York, Anchor Books, 2005.

Hattaway, Michael. *The Cambridge Companion to Shakespeare's History Plays.* Cambridge ; New York ; Melbourne, Cambridge University Press, 2009.

Hoenselaars, A J. *The Cambridge Companion to Shakespeare and Contemporary Dramatists.* Cambridge England ; New York, Cambridge University Press, 2012.

Leggatt, Alexander. *The Cambridge Companion to Shakespearean Comedy.* Cambridge ; New York ; Melbourne, Cambridge University Press, 2010.

Magnusson, Lynne, and David Schalkwyk. *The Cambridge Companion to Shakespeare's Language.* Cambridge, United Kingdom ; New York, Ny, Cambridge University Press, 2019.

Margreta De Grazia, and Stanley W Wells. *The New Cambridge Companion to Shakespeare.* New York, Cambridge University Press, 2010.

Mceachern, Claire. *The Cambridge Companion to Shakespearean Tragedy.* Cambridge, United Kingdom, Cambridge University Press, 2013.

Palfrey, Simon, and Tiffany Stern. *Shakespeare in Parts.* Oxford ; New York, Oxford University Press, 2007.

Shakespeare, William. *The Illustrated Stratford Shakespeare.* London, Bounty Books, 2009.

Shapiro, James. *1606 : William Shakespeare and the Year of Lear.* London, Faber & Faber, 2016.

---. *A Year in the Life of William Shakespeare, 1599.* New York, Harper Perennial, 2006.

---. *Contested Will : Who Wrote Shakespeare?* New York, Simon & Schuster, 2011.

Stern, Tiffany. *Making Shakespeare : From Stage to Print.* London, Routledge, 2004.

Vickers, Brian. *Shakespeare, Co-Author.* Oxford University Press, 2004.

William Shakespeare a Midsummer Night's Dream. Directed by Dominic Dromgoole and Shakespeare's Globe, Opus Arte, 2014.

William Shakespeare Antony and Cleopatra. Directed by Iqbal Khan and RSC, Opus Arte, 2018.

William Shakespeare As You like It. Directed by Kimberly Sykes and RSC, Opus Arte, 2020.

William Shakespeare As You like It. Directed by Thea Sharrok and Globe Theatre, Opus Arte, 2010.

William Shakespeare Coriolanus. Directed by Angus Jackson and RSC, Opus Arte, 2018.

William Shakespeare Hamlet. Directed by Simon Godwin and RSC, Opus Arte, 2016.

William Shakespeare Henry IV Part 1. Directed by Dominic Dromgoole and Globe Theatre, Opus Arte, 2012.

William Shakespeare Henry IV Part 1. Directed by Gregory Dorian and RSC, Opus Arte, 2016.

William Shakespeare Henry IV Part 2. Directed by Dominic Dromgoole and Globe Theatre, Opus Arte, 2012.

William Shakespeare Henry IV Part 2. Directed by Gregory Dorian and RSC, Opus Arte, 2016.

William Shakespeare Henry V. Directed by Dominic Dromgoole and Globe Theatre, Opus Arte, 2013.

William Shakespeare Henry V. Directed by Gregory Dorian and RSC, Opus Arte, 2016.

William Shakespeare Julius Caesar. Directed by Angus Jackson and RSC, Opus Arte, 2018.

William Shakespeare Julius Caesar. Directed by Dominic Dromgoole and Globe Theatre, Opus Arte, 2015.

William Shakespeare King Lear. Directed by Gregory Dorian and RSC, Opus Arte, 2016.
William Shakespeare Macbeth. Directed by Gregory Dorian and RSC, Opus Arte, 2019.
William Shakespeare Measure for Measure. Directed by Gregory Dorian and RSC, Opus Arte, 2019.
William Shakespeare Much Ado about Nothing. Directed by Christopher Luscombe and RSC, Opus Arte, 2015.
William Shakespeare Othello. Directed by Iqbal Kahn and RSC, Opus Arte, 2015.
William Shakespeare Richard II. Directed by Gregory Dorian and RSC, Opus Arte, 2016.
William Shakespeare Romeo and Juliet. Directed by Dominic Dromgoole and Globe Theatre, Opus Arte, 2010.
William Shakespeare the Taming of the Shrew. Directed by Justin Audibert and RSC, Opus Arte, 2019.
William Shakespeare the Taming of the Shrew. Directed by Toby Frow and Globe Theatre, Opus Arte, 2013.
William Shakespeare Titus Andronicus. Directed by Blanche McIntyre and RSC, Opus Arte, 2018.
William Shakespeare Twelfth Night. Directed by Tim Carroll and Globe Theatre, Opus Arte, 2013.
William Shakespeare's Antony and Cleopatra. Directed by Jonathan Munby and Globe Theatre, Opus Arte, 2015.

Glossary

A
abatement – lessening
abhorr'd – loathe, disgust, reject
adieu – a farewell
afeared – afraid or frightened
ague – fever or sickness
alarum – urged on
anon – soon or shortly
apish – silly or foolish
arrant – absolute
attest – vouch for, testify to

B
base – dishonourable, unworthy, low
belike – probably, perhaps
blench – flinch, start or shrink
bootless – useless, worthless
bully – excellent (form of address)
by'r lakin – our Lady (swearing)

C
canoniz'd – glorify, immortalise
cerements – grave clothes, waxed shroud
choler – anger, rage
cloy – gorge, satisfy
community – commonness, familiarity, acquaintance
condole – lament, grieve
com'st – comes
conjure – ask solemnly, beseech
corrival – equal, match
cote – cottage
coted – overtake or pass by
coxcomb – a jester's crested cap
cozeners – cheat, fraud
cranny – crack, split

D
dissembly - malapropism means assembly
divers-coloured – many coloured
doth – do
drave – drove
dubb'd – named

E

eftest – malapropism means quickest
entreated – persuaded, plea

F

falchion – curved broadsword
fancy-monger – love-dealer
fell – cruel, savage deadly or destructive
fly – run away, flee or attack furiously
forsooth – in truth, truly, indeed
forswear – abandon, renounce
fustian – made up in a ridiculous way

G

gall – vex, irritate
galled – sore, swollen, inflamed

H

hazard – risk, take a chance
hempen – made of hemp
hie – hurry up or speed up
hither – here
hose – men's stocking

I

incarnadine – turn blood red
inductions – opening scenes
indued – endowed, supplied
inure – accustom, adapt
inurn'd – bury

J

John-a-dreams – dreamer

K

knave – rascal, scoundrel, rogue or boy
knavery – roguish trick, treachery

L

lay – song
Lenten – made in Lent (Lent is the six week period before Easter in the Christian calendar)
lett – hinder, obstacle
lour'd – frown, scowl
love-shak'd – love sick

M

malefactions – criminal act, evil doings
marry – by Mary (swearing)
masquers – participants at a masquerade
mean – low rank, humble, unimportant
methinks – it seems to me
mew'd – confined
mischance – misfortune
missives – messages
mourning-weeds – mourning clothes

N

necessity – unavoidable event
niggardly – miserly, tightfisted, skinflint
nott-pated – short haired

O

odious – malapropism means odours
O'er – over
O'erhang – over hang
o'erpicturing - surpass, outdo, excel
o'erposting - disregard, overlook
o'erwhelmed – over whelmed
ope – open
opinioned – malapropism for pinioned – tied up or bound
ordinary – everyday, commonplace
outwork – excel in workmanship

P

parlous – dangerous, hazardous
pate – head
perchance – perhaps, maybe
physic – cure, correct
portage – portholes, opening
prithee – please
proffer – offer, proposal
prythee – please (different spelling)

Q

quintessence – purest form

R

redemption – rescue
revels – party, make merry
riggish – lascivious, wanton

S

savours – scent, smell
score – twenty
sirrah – sir
sooth – truly
spoil – plunder, booty
staniel – inferior kind of hawk
starveling – skinny or lanky person
straitly – strictly, firmly
strange – aloof, distant, reserved
strappado – a torture device

T

ta'en - taken
tallow-keech – a lump of congealed animal fat
tempest – storm
thence – away from there
tuck – long slender sword

U

unbanded – without a coloured hatband
ungarter – not wearing garters. Bands worn below the knee to hold up hose

V

varlet – rogue, knave, ruffian
visage – face

W

wan – turn pale
wanton – wilful or obstinate individual.
wench – affectionate form of address to a close female relative or wife
whoreson – bastard, vile, wretched
worn – exhausted

Y

yarely – quickly, briskly
yond – there
yonder – that over there

Z

zounds – god's wounds (swearing)

About the Author

Natalie Muller is a writer, teacher and founder of Black Cockie Press specialising in new Australian writing. She holds a Master of Arts in Writing from Swinburne University of Technology. Natalie has taught in New South Wales schools for over two decades, and has also taught Creative Writing through WEA Sydney and privately. Between 2014 – 2019 Natalie developed, piloted and implemented the Editor- in-Residence program through the BMCC Library. Natalie also presents and produces a weekly literary themed YouTube channel under the title Black Cockie Press.

www.ingramcontent.com/pod-product-compliance
Lightning Source LLC
Chambersburg PA
CBHW061537010526
44107CB00067B/2897